T0166486

AFTER CANAAN

AFTER CANAAN

Essays on Race, Writing, and Region

WAYDE COMPTON

Arsenal Pulp Press
Vancouver

ARSENAL PULP PRESS
Suite 101, 211 East Georgia St.
Vancouver, BC
Canada V6A 1Z6
arsenalpulp.com

The publisher gratefully acknowledges the support of the Canada Council for the Arts and the British Columbia Arts Council for its publishing program, and the Government of Canada through the Canada Book Fund and the Government of British Columbia through the Book Publishing Tax Credit Program for its publishing activities.

Cover photograph: Digital reproduction of Hogan's Alley by Stan Douglas
Author photograph by Lani Russwurm

Printed and bound in Canada

Library and Archives Canada Cataloguing in Publication

Compton, Wayde, 1972-
    After Canaan : essays on race, writing, and region / Wayde Compton.

Includes index.
Issued also in electronic fromat.
ISBN 978-1-55152-374-3

    1. Post-racialism—Canada. 2. Multiculturalism—Canada.
3. Race in literature. 4. Canada—Intellectual life—20th century.
I. Title.

FC104.C645 2010   305.800971   C2010-904253-0

CONTENTS

Everything flows and nothing abides;
everything gives way and nothing stays fixed.
—Heraclitus (ca. 535–ca. 475)

Over there we'll shout, "Trouble's over!"
Over there we'll shout, "Trouble's over!"
With the angels singing
And the joybell ringing
And glory—
Lord, how far am I from Canaan?
—Rev. W. Herbert Brewster (1897–1987)

For Anne and Senna, my beautiful ones.

ACKNOWLEDGMENTS

Thanks to Anthony Ekundayo Lennon, Rhonda Larrabee, Fred Wah, David Chariandy, Anne Stone, and Mark D. Engstrom for their support and assistance during the writing of "Pheneticizing Versus Passing."

The seed of "Blackvoice and Stately Ways: Isaac Dickson, Mifflin Gibbs, and Black British Columbia's First Trials of Authenticity" was a lecture I was commissioned to do for the Kootenay School of Writing's "Time Mechanix" series on June 5, 2001. Thanks to Reg Johanson and the KSW for this prompt. I expanded and revised a version of the lecture for the University of Victoria's "Untold Stories of British Columbia" conference on March 1–2, 2002; it was published in a collection of papers from that conference in 2003, edited by Paul Wood, to whom I also owe thanks.

Versions of "Seven Routes to Hogan's Alley and Vancouver's Black Community" first appeared in *West Coast LINE* 47 (2005), in the program for the Under the Volcano festival in 2007, and in *Multiple Lenses: Voices From the Diaspora Located in Canada* (2007), a collection of papers from the conference of the same name at Dalhousie University in Halifax, Nova Scotia (October 26–28, 2005). Thanks go to all the editors and organizers of these events and publications. Much of the research at the heart of this essay was a collective effort that includes the work of my fellow members of the Hogan's Alley Memorial Project (HAMP), past and present, including Sheilagh Cahill, Junie Désil, Naomi Moyer, Adam Rudder, Joy Russell, and Karina Vernon. The Vancouver Public Library and the City of Vancouver Archives have also been extremely helpful in bringing attention to Hogan's Alley and Vancouver's early black community. Lauren Marsden's art installation "Hogan's Alley Welcomes You"—a guerrilla gardening plot created in tandem with HAMP, and mentioned in this essay—was an exhilarating experiment lateral to the regular archival process. Heather MacDonald's research assistance in the final stages of crafting this essay was indispensable. James Johnstone also generously helped me with fact-checking and additional research regarding the presence of the black porters and the Militant Mothers of Raymur in and near the neighbourhood. Thelma Gibson, Tracey Macdougall, Brenda Crump, and the members of the Basel Hakka Lutheran Church all generously shared information, memories, and glimpses into their roles in the history of this neighbourhood. Thanks to all these wonderful people.

Thanks to Monique Gingras for support in the writing of "The Repossession of Fred Booker."

"Alexis Mazurin, the Hot Sauce Posse, and Black History Month on the Edge" first appeared in the web magazine *The Tyee* (February 15, 2006). Thanks to David Beers and Vanessa Richmond for editing it. Thanks also go to the members of the Hot Sauce Posse, and in particular Charlie Cho and Tetsuro Shigematsu, for insight into Mazurin's legacy.

"Turntable Poetry, Mixed-Race, and Schizophonophilia" was first written for the "Games We Play: Strategies of the Everyday" conference at Simon Fraser University, May 9–11,

2008, though it borrows some elements from previous essays titled "The Reinventing Wheel: On Blending the Poetry of Cultures Through Hip Hop Turntablism," published in the web magazine *Horizon Zero* 8 (2003), and "Out Here a Minute: The Biracial Local, By Ear," which appeared in *Event* 32.1 (Spring 2003). Thanks to the organizers and editors of all three for including me in their projects. And thanks to Jason de Couto and Trevor Thompson for the ongoing conversations through sound.

Belinda Bruce deserves thanks for providing diligent research assistance for "Obama and Language."

Special thanks to Stan Douglas for generously providing the cover image for this book.

I taught four cycles of the Narrative and Non-Fiction workshop at The Writers' Studio, Continuing Studies, Simon Fraser University (2006–09), and I learned a great deal there, through the two-way pedagogical door of Harbour Centre. Thanks to Betsy Warland, the director, and thanks to all my mentees, for helping to make me a better writer.

In a similar regard, thanks to Anne Stone and David Chariandy for reading early drafts of these essays and pointing out ways to improve them.

Thanks to Joe and Audrey at the Bump N Grind Café in Vancouver, where I wrote and edited much of the final draft of this book.

Thanks to all the folks at Arsenal Pulp Press—Brian Lam, Robert Ballantyne, Shyla Seller, Susan Safyan, and Janice Beley—for making it happen.

And, finally, I am pleased to acknowledge the generous support of the Simon Fraser University Writer-in-Residence program, which gave me time and resources to write during the 2007–08 season. I also gratefully acknowledge the reception of a grant from the British Columbia Arts Council which was applied to the last stages of this project.

INTRODUCTION

Western Canada may seem an unlikely place from which to write about black culture and identity—a space with a relatively small population of African descent, whose history has barely penetrated the national or international consciousness. All the more reason: here, where black history and cultural legacy need recuperation, acts of recovery that return a more complete picture of the place broaden everyone's purview. But even within the conceptual bounds of the African diaspora itself, I believe that looking to the margins rather than the centres has a unique value; that there are things to be learned from owning and exploring oblique kinds of blackness. In the periphery, where there are fewer local expectations of what "the black experience" ought to be, radical experiments of identity can be tried. And where the standard continental systems of anti-black racism have been unevenly applied, new systems of thought against racism might be expected to emerge.

An anecdote: in January 2008, on the day of Barack Obama's inauguration as the US president, a reporter phoned me seeking comments from black community members in British

Columbia, asking what, if anything, this victory meant to black Canadians from the west. I was holding my two-month-old daughter in my arms at the time, cradling her while cradling the phone with my shoulder, distracted and focused on first-time fatherhood. I mumbled a few of the clichés that were in the air. It meant "change" and it meant "hope." The reporter had been hearing this all day, I imagine, and she pushed me. "Yes, yes, but what does it mean for blacks *here*?" And it hit me that though Obama's win is a foreign event, and therefore somewhat abstract to Canadians, we nevertheless may have a more intimate identification with him than most black Americans do. Because, much like him, our experience here is one of being outside the diasporic master narratives: our communities developed beyond the sites of slavery; interracial families are our standard experience rather than an exceptional or suspect one; our dialect is the same as the dominant society ("Standard English"); and though there are old black families in BC, a great many of us are immigrants or the children of them. This set of circumstances at the outer rim of black centres means we are, to some degree, in charge of our own enculturation. And so the experience Obama describes in *Dreams from My Father* (1995), of growing up and piecing together his black identity from a mix of popular culture representations, books, and fleeting encounters with other blacks, is familiar; in addition, the demographic similarity between his Hawaii and our BC—places defined by their Indigenous and Asian minorities rather than blacks—extends the corollary. Embracing this set of unusual black experiences, rather than trying to return to the imagined essence of a past blackness, is, for me, an assertive Afroperipheralism—in contrast to the redemptive drive of Afrocentrism, which iterates everything but a narrow set of perceived traditions as inauthentic and culturally ersatz.

This is not to say that our experience is altogether beyond the paths of the greater diaspora. Where the links are conceptual, they are nevertheless tangible, and the experience here has long been defined by and against a bigger, continental historical saga. For example, in the mythos of the African-American spirituals, the psalmic land of longing and the home of the captured Israelites was Canaan—the north, the land of salvation, sometimes bound together with the idea of an eternal afterlife. As Frederick Douglass wrote in *My Bondage and My Freedom* (1855), "We were, at times, remarkably buoyant, singing hymns and making joyous exclamations, almost as triumphant in their tone as if we reached a land of freedom and safety. A keen observer might have detected in our repeated singing of 'O Canaan, sweet Canaan, / I am bound for the land of Canaan,' something more than a hope of reaching heaven. We meant to reach the north—and the north was our Canaan." It was also, oftentimes, the place beyond the northern states— Canada, encoded—the haven of British jurisdiction where slavery had been abolished a generation earlier than in the US. It is one of the grand allegories of the diaspora: the flight north, the crossing of the Jordan, the claiming of home.

But for the blacks who fled to Canada, the spectacular allegory hardened into a cold prosody upon arrival, and for those who had been enslaved in Canada, the allegory was an empty

sign from the very start. Nevertheless, this is one of the symbolic legacies of black Canada—to be the appendix of the epic and
the echo of the odyssey. For slaves and free immigrants alike,
Canaan/Canada is a supposed site of magical transformation.
Scholar Alyssa MacLean notes how "the water imagery of
Lake Erie linked Canadian-American cross-border narratives
to a well-established genre in the US" where "[s]lave narratives
had long represented slavery as a form of social death, a kind
of political drowning or suffocation." MacLean goes on to
paraphrase critic Shelly Rosenblum, suggesting that "the passage through rivers in US slave narratives often symbolized a
form of baptism, or the death of a slave subject and the rebirth
of a person" (2009, 4). And on the west coast, too, historian
Crawford Kilian tells of Charles Mitchell, a slave who stowed
away aboard a US ship bound for Victoria in 1860. The ship's
captain caught Mitchell en route and locked him up on board,
intending to give him back to his owner when the ship returned
to an American port. But Victoria's black community found
out about Mitchell's presence and managed to get him removed
from the ship and into police custody. While there was some
debate about the legality of removing him from the ship, it was
successfully argued that "the mere presence of Charles Mitchell on British soil made him *ipso facto* a free man," and he was
released (Kilian 2008, 66–67). To get to Canaan is to erase
the tribulation of the past. To merely touch its soil is to receive
redemption, as if this region were replete with a benevolent
kind of contagion. So a local claim on this space is intertwined
with demystifying the symbolic order of those narratives, and

rewriting a northern actuality. And yet, being an afterthought minority has left open a modicum of space for self-definition— if, that is, one can take it as an exhilarating opportunity rather than a deficiency. This complicated terrain is the site and specification of our writing and resistance.

The essays herein speak to multiple issues: the fallacious language of mixed-race; the historical scrutiny of black discourse; the experience of a hostile urban renewal; elegies to cultural producers who resisted racial categorization; the literary potential of hip hop; and an examination of the Obama phenomenon as it transforms language. These essays were originally written between 2000 and 2010, often for various journals and conferences, but some specifically for this volume. The common spirit binding them is, I hope, a cultural recovery and advocacy that is, in Paul Gilroy's phrasing, "the restoration of political culture" as opposed to "raciology's destructive claims upon the very best of modernity's hopes and resources" (2000, 30). Rather than the old narratives of escape, uplift, and redemption—which need to be re-thought and freshened—I hope to contribute to the projects of multiculturalism-from-below and counter-canonicity. Where I am agnostic about the spirituals—that golden inheritance—what I put my faith in here is the empowered subject formation that comes after strategic essentialism and unreconstructed identity politics.

PHENETICIZING VERSUS PASSING

SUBJECT-VERB-RACE

To open up a discussion of the term "passing" and its limitations, I want to look first at an essay by Shane Book called "Border Crossings," excerpted in *Geist* in 1999. In this short serial memoir, largely concerned with his experiences of racialization, Book describes himself as "Dutch-Irish-German-American from Manitoba" on his father's side with a mother from Trinidad whose family is "mostly black, except for one of her grandparents being Chinese and someone back there, Spanish with some Caribe Indian mixed in" (27). Nevertheless, during his travels throughout North America, Book finds himself at various times stopped and questioned by police and border guards, and in each of these cases his ancestry is perceived by these agents of authority according to the region and its particular racial anxieties: in Manitoba, a police officer tries to direct him to the North End of Winnipeg "where all the Indians live"; at the Windsor–Detroit border, the fact that the author was born in Peru—an "accident," he explains, as both of his parents were Canadians temporarily working there at the time—causes the guard to believe he is ethnically Peruvian (25); at the Peace Arch border in British Columbia, the author is assumed to be an itinerant "Hispanic" fruit picker; another police officer in Washington State, who once lived in the South Pacific, is convinced that Book is Samoan; at the Arizona-California border, a highway patrolman keeps asking him if he is Mexican; and on the Golden Gate Bridge, where Book is site-seeing outside of hours, guards stop and ask him if he has "any affiliation with the Middle East" and if he speaks Arabic (25–27). What is typical about Book's experience is the number of times this law-abiding man of African descent gets stopped by officials. But what makes it an interesting statement on the mixed-race experience is the fact that none of these officials correctly determine his actual background, but rather attribute their own preferred back-stories to his enigmatically brown appearance.

The English language has only one word to specifically describe the phenomenon Book experiences—we call it "passing"; we say Book, in each of these incidents, "passed" for Indian, Peruvian, Hispanic, Samoan, Mexican, or Arab. The origins of the term lie in the American "one-drop rule," the historical policy of segregation that defined as black those who had *any* degree of known African ancestry—one drop of "Negro blood" was enough to classify one as black. In this asymmetrical social definition of miscegenation, all mixed offspring were black, and so were their children, and their children's children. Only those who were "purely" white were white at all.[1] This policy—which, it might be added for comparison, was stricter than the Nazis' anti-Semitic, anti-miscegenation laws—led to the inevitable situation in which people who had far more white ancestry than black were socially and legally defined as black. To put a finer point on it, under this system, some people who looked white were, nevertheless, socially and legally black. Such persons who decided to defy this definition and live instead as whites could do so only by lying about their family background or omitting mention of any black ancestors, a process which usually also required disassociation with family members. This act came to be known as "passing"—meaning that the individual, when tested by an inquisitive viewer's gaze, could get away with the crime of racial self-assignment.

Although the term "passing" is rooted in the context of the American Reconstruction, it continues to be used today and has become a part of the English language internationally. Its meaning has also been expanded to encompass any kind of racial transposition, whether deliberate or not. A person with mixed Polish and Burmese ancestry living in Ireland, for example, might be said to "pass" for Roma if locals see him or her that way at first glance. The term has also advanced beyond the racial context, and those who transcend gender or class identities also sometimes describe their experience as "passing." And Shane Book, writing about his travels across North America, might be said to have written a contemporary "passing narrative"—a story in which he moves in and out of different racial categories.

The essential problem with the term, however, is that it illogically implies that what a viewer sees is the responsibility of the person being seen. That is to say, this term we have for phenomena of misrecognition always implies deception on the part of the individual viewed. At its root, the term is about getting away with it, going underground, and intentionally escaping an oppressive racializing order. But what of those circumstances in which the person viewed has made no comment or projection of any kind, but rather is simply read by a viewer? In Book's case, for example, one might find oneself saying, "When he was in the US, Book passed for Mexican." But the syntax is misleading; the active voice steers us wrong. He *did* nothing. Rather, Book had something *done to him* when the highway patrolman racially appraised him. Whatever the etymological origins of the term—Baz Dreisinger suggests that it is either short for "trespassing" or refers to the written passes that slaves were given by their owners to travel (2008, 4)—"passing" grammatically absents the person who reads someone's race. In the sentence, "Book passed for Mexican," there is no highway patrolman. Yet it is far more correct to say that the patrolman acted—that he perceived or misperceived Book. He saw Book as Mexican, wholly apart from anything Book might have done to appear one way or another.

The subject of this essay is the proposal of a corrective to this lapse in our socially directed language. If we stop saying, "Book passed for Mexican," what do we say instead that the patrolman did? What speech act did the man with a badge and a motorcycle commit that day at the side of the road near the Arizona-California border?

But first, why does this matter? While it is easy to demonstrate that the language is not exact, does this matter enough to necessitate a new term altogether? Because the word "passing" is rooted in deception, I would argue that, yes, we do need another term when deception is not being committed during an act of racial misperception, otherwise the impression will be left—if only subconsciously—that racial misperception is always the fault of the object. This predisposition to make the *viewed* responsible for what the *viewer* sees, reinforced by such inexact terminology, locks together dangerously with prejudices already in play against mixed-race people, who are often seen as inherently destabilizing, ambivalent, or disloyal by definition. Therefore, when a person with mixed Cree and Norweigan ancestry, for example, walks down the street and is seen by someone who assumes she is only white, our inadequate phraseology—that she is "passing for white"—is much like saying that because a man finds a woman attractive, she is flirting with him. Both formulations are dangerous for the way that they lift the viewer wholly out of any implication and responsibility.

And so we need a new term that corrects this logical fallacy. We can borrow a word from biology—"phenetics"—and adapt it to this social phenomenon, recasting its verb form to create an alternative term, "pheneticizing."

Phenetics (phenetic taxonomy) is "the classification of organisms on the basis of their observed similarities and differences (often assessed in numerical terms), without reference to functional significance or evolutionary relationships" (*OED Online*, s.v. "Phenetic"). It is contrasted with and has largely been replaced by "cladistics" in biological theory, which is the "systematic classification of groups of organisms on the basis of shared characteristics thought to derive from a common ancestor" (*OED Online*, s.v. "Cladistics"). In other words, phenetics, which comes from a school of thought that is falling out of favour, assigns biological classification based on outward appearance to the eye, whereas cladistics, a method from an ascendant school of thought, favours classification based on the background of evolutionary development. The metaphor should be clear: pheneticizing, in my definition, is the classification of a person's race or ethnicity based only on eyeball examination, rather than the cladisitic inquiry that would require knowing the person's actual family background.[2]

Of course, in cases where someone *does* consciously pose as some racial or cultural group to which he or she has no connection, then the word "passing" should be used as the term. But only then, when the individual is being deliberately deceptive or subversive and intentionally adopts another ancestry. It is important to note, though, that such deception or subversion is not necessarily morally wrong. Whether or not one has the *right* to transgress one's racial designation surely depends upon the perniciousness of the regime that is policing the designations. Some of the complex situational ethics behind decisions to pass will be discussed through examples in the third section of this essay.

A VERY SHORT GLOSSARY OF RACIAL TRANSGRESSION

cladisticizing: Racially perceiving someone by inquiring into his or her family history.

passing: Deliberately misrepresenting oneself racially.

pheneticizing: Racially perceiving someone based on a subjective examination of his or her outward appearance.

phenopolysemic: A person whose appearance can suggest more than one racial designation.

race: A folk taxonomy; a pseudo-scientific demographic categorization system. Like a national border or literary genre, race is only as real as our current social consensus.

A CIRCLE OF RACIAL TRANSGRESSIONS

Going beyond definition-building, I want to apply the idea of pheneticization to four case studies. The experiment here is to inject the verb "pheneticize" and the noun "phenetics" into these erstwhile "passing narratives," to see if a different interpretation of events emerges through the new phrasing.

But while we are doing so, I also want to create a circular series of exegeses, for a further function. Because the originating situation that occasioned the term "passing" was so racially and regionally specific (regarding American, and usually Southern, mixed-race blacks integrating into white society), I want to widen this new discussion, tracing a circle of transgressive experiences in which one identity formation collapses into another and another in succession, until we arrive back at the first—a circle of racial transgressions in which an ostensibly black person becomes Native, a Native person becomes Asian, an Asian person becomes white, and a white person becomes black:

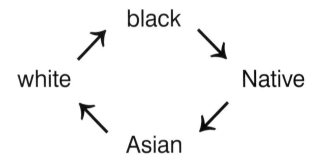

A circle of racial transgressions.

This method, I think, will help to do away with any standardizing myths of a one-way "vertical" progression (black to white), and the circular structuring of the problem will also intimate a sense of futility inherent in notions of race—a gesture toward the idea that all motions into, out of, and through race reside within a system, a loop, a locked groove; to illustrate how the myth of race indeed chases itself.

BLACK TO NATIVE: CHIEF BUFFALO CHILD LONG LANCE

While the race of the man who called himself Chief Buffalo Child Long Lance has been a subject of debate and remains inconclusive, because his life (and death) were largely determined by his flight from classification as black and toward being seen as Native, I will situate his story as a "black to Native" narrative of racial transgression. Indeed, when Sylvester Long (his legal name at birth) was born in 1890 to Sallie and Joseph Long in Winston, North Carolina, his family, under the conditions of Southern segregation, were socially and legally categorized as black. However, at the age of nineteen, Long applied to the Carlisle Indian School, a US residential institution, on the basis of the Native ancestry that his parents claimed. Because his mother's ancestry was part Lumbee Indian—an affiliation that was itself formed out of multiple "[t]ribal groups along the Atlantic coast [that] had been splintered beyond recognition after the massive arrival of Europeans"—and his father could not prove his own claim as part Cherokee, the Long family's Native status was considered ambiguous (D. Smith 1999, 40–41). But in order to gain admission to Carlisle, Long had to prove to them that he was at least a quarter Native. To do this, he was forced to obtain vouchers from two prominent local citizens of Winston, saying he was indeed Native; he also had to pass a linguistic test at the school, which he did, shakily, by speaking a few phrases of Cherokee he had learned while working in a "wild west" show in a local circus a few years earlier. From this point forward in Long's life, his authenticity as a Native person was repeatedly challenged, and he increasingly moved to answer these challenges by stretching the truth about his ancestry more and more. He began to claim that he was a full-blood, omitting that he had white ancestry, and suppressing the fact that his family was known at home as having black roots as well. At the end of his life, Long Lance—as he came to style himself—had unilaterally taken on the mantle of chief, had adopted a Blackfoot identity, had placed his birth thousands of miles away from where he was actually born, and had created a Native identity for himself that little resembled his documented background. The Native person he chose to become was, in many ways, a reflection of white society's vision of the romantic, tragic, "noble savage"—and he used the margin of favour that this vision afforded, rather than the abjection of black and Native realities, to travel in social circles far above the station that a black man of North Carolina could have otherwise expected.

Despite this imposture, there was genuine acceptance that Long Lance was Native, at least in part: his recommendation to the Carlisle school came first from a white school principal in Winston, who viewed the Longs as having Native blood, and he was able to obtain testimonies from both white and black pillars of the community when he needed it (D. Smith 1999, 40–41). So the fact that he was Native, to some degree, has never been in question. The problem was that, though both Long Lance's parents considered themselves admixtures of white and Native (13, 27), there was a suspicion that they were part black. And in North Carolina at that time, the one-drop rule was law. A person with any known black ancestry was black, regardless of how small the fraction—one-fourth, one-eighth, one-sixteenth, and so on. What is most curious is that, for the Longs, it was not *known* black ancestry that served to classify them so—it was merely the inability to prove they were *not* black. The fact that both Sallie and Joseph Long had ancestors who were slaves—even though Indian enslavement was common in earlier generations in the American South—coupled with their ambiguous colouring, was enough to put the suggestion of blackness upon them. And it is here where Long Lance's story becomes one not only of passing, but of pheneticization.

It is certain that Long Lance passed—though when exactly you pinpoint his moment of deception depends on your idea of what constitutes Native authenticity. Is it accurate to say that he was "passing for Native" when he really did have Native blood? Or was he merely creating his own sort of one-drop rule, favouring Native identity rather than black? Later in his life, when he was posing as a Blackfoot, it is possible to think of this as merely ethnic, rather than racial, passing—a Lumbee/Cherokee pretending to be a different sort of Native—which is indeed how his publisher, upon discovering that his autobiography was bogus, viewed it (D. Smith 1999, 284). Maybe he was merely trading an eastern Native identity for a western one.

Where pheneticization enters as a useful term of clarification in Long Lance's story is at the curious moment when his parents became black, before Long Lance was even born. In

Sallie and Joseph Long. Photo: Glenbow Museum, NA-3771-1

Chief Buffalo Child Long Lance (McDermid Studios, Edmonton, Alberta.) Photo: Glenbow Musem, NA-177-1

Long Lance's biography, Donald B. Smith recounts how when, in the 1880s, the Longs first moved to Winston from Carson Town, they presented themselves as what they always claimed to be, each a mix of Native and white. But their social and legal racialization, in this new town, came to depend on a messy swirl of local knowledge, demographic precedents for comparison, and what I call pheneticization: a contemporary of the Longs reported that Joseph "was understood as Indian" and the Longs "were advised to act as such" when they first moved to Winston—and "acting as such" meant avoiding the black community and associating themselves with the few local families who were mixed white and Native (1999, 280). But because there were few of the latter, Smith believes the local white townsfolk of Winston in the late nineteenth century saw people as only either black or white, and those few locals who had known traces of Native blood were considered basically white. It was when the Longs tried to attend a white church and the congregation rejected them that their classification became fixed. Sallie alone might have made it as white, but Joseph's skin was considered too dark, and so the Longs were collectively branded as black for the rest of their lives thereafter (281–83). In the segregated site of the church, the Longs' status was put to the test, and though by the one-drop rule's own precepts they were not black, in that room on that Sunday, pheneticization carried the day. Joseph looked too much like he *might* be black, and that was that.

Toward the end of his life, Long Lance's fabrications caught up with him. After the publication of his false autobiography, investigations into his background turned up his early classification as black, and he was again publicly regarded as such. Many of the friends he had made as an "Indian chief" (whose achievements included an honourable war record in the Canadian Army during World War I, a starring role in the film *The Silent Enemy: An Epic of the American Indian* [1929]), a sports shoe endorsement deal, and the book contract) abandoned him when his origins were discovered. Smith writes that Irvin S. Cobb, an erstwhile friend of Long Lance who wrote the foreword to his memoir, "exploded in anger" when he heard that Long Lance was part black: "To think that we had him here in the house," Cobb exclaimed. "We're so ashamed! We entertained a nigger [...]" (D. Smith 1999, 273). In the end, Long Lance committed suicide, shooting himself in the head in Los Angeles in 1932 in the wake of these events.

But the question remains: what exactly *were* Long Lance's transgressions? He was no chief and he was no Blackfoot. But was he a black man? We only know how his father was seen—the cast of his skin, the width of his nose—by a small number of townsfolk in a racially paranoid place and time. Joseph Long was too dark and his features too polysemic, so society erred on the side of blackness. And whereas the father accepted this summary racial designation, refusing to relocate his family elsewhere in order to try to shake it off, the son rebelled. Knowing his father's experience, Long Lance based his life of misrepresentations on the lesson learned that day when the Longs were barred from Winston's white church. He passed in order to intercept a roaming pheneticization that he knew could demote one suddenly, firmly, and forever. Long Lance's passing was a matter of the best defence being a good offence against an opposing urge to round down any racial indecipherability to occult Africanity.

NATIVE TO ASIAN: RHONDA LARRABEE

In the previous description of Long Lance's life, one might wonder at the idea of finding better fortune as a Native than as a person of African descent. Indeed, the history of the Native side of Long Lance's family shows they enjoyed no greater status than blacks had: his Lumbee and Cherokee ancestors in fact suffered slavery, deportation, plague, and genocide. And the Natives that Long Lance encountered in his travels throughout North America continued to live in conditions that were poor; they were socially outcast and desperate, often experiencing their own sort of segregation on reserves (in Canada) and reservations (in the US). As I noted, Long Lance was able to elevate himself only in the guise of the most white-friendly and romantic image of a Native person that he could conjure, making of himself a popular spectacle. At the end of his autobiography-fable, Long Lance's conclusion shows the sort of accommodating Native he had become; his final paragraph breezily sweeps aside Native suffering, insisting that "the new day is here: it is here to stay. And now we must leave it to our old people to sit stolidly and dream of the glories of our past. Our job is to try to fit ourselves into the new scheme of life which the Great Spirit has decreed for North America. And we will do that, keeping always before us the old Blackfoot proverb: *Mokokit-ki-acka-*

mimat—Be wise and persevere" (1956, 241). But in other times and places—as the story of Rhonda Larrabee shows—escaping anti-Native racism was just as desperate a prospect as getting away from black segregation was for Long Lance. In the documentary film *A Tribe of One* (2003), filmmaker Eunhee Cha shows us how Larrabee's family transgressed racial boundaries in a way that is similar to Long Lance's experience, but they moved from Native identification to Chinese, and back again, in Vancouver, BC.

In the film, which is largely a series of interviews with Larrabee and members of her family, a story emerges in which the New Westminster Indian Band—now known as the Qayqayt First Nation—were assessed in 1913 by a Canadian royal commission as too small for official recognition after having been ravaged by small pox during the late nineteenth century. Because there were only about a hundred members of the tribe left, they were legally deregistered and expected to assimilate into other local First Nations. Larrabee's mother, Marie Joseph, was a member of this band, born on their reserve but sent to the Kamloops Residential School far away in the interior of BC when she was a child. This history of double erasure—of suffering both the assimilationist horror of the Canadian residential school system, as well as the dismantling of her band—goes a long way in explaining why Marie decided to adopt another identity after she left residential school and found herself on the streets of Vancouver's East End. After getting a job as a waitress in Chinatown, Marie discovered that people sometimes mistook her for Asian. So after marrying

Art Lee, a Chinese Canadian, she began to pass for Eurasian, claiming a mix of Chinese and French ancestry. Marie Lee kept her true identity secret even from her own children, who grew up believing they were three-quarters Chinese and one-quarter French. It was not until her daughter, Rhonda, was twenty-four years old that Marie finally confessed her actual maternal lineage; she reluctantly spoke of it to her daughter only that one time, and never mentioned it again.

Thereafter the story takes a remarkable and redemptive turn. During a quest to discover more about her suppressed roots, Rhonda Larrabee successfully applied to have herself registered as a "status Indian" and, realizing that her band was still officially unrecognized, began a process to have the Qayqayt once again registered by the Canadian government. While going through this process, Larrabee encouraged her brothers and other family members to apply for their official status as well and, realizing that the band needed a chief to fulfill official requirements, found herself voted in as the first chief, since the 1913 ruling, of the newly revived Qayqayt First Nation. And so Larrabee, far from living out her mother's intended legacy of passing, instead became a leader in an epic revival of this small nation, taking it from the brink of annihilation to a renaissance—although, as is noted in the film, the Qayqayt still have not (as of 2010) recovered their land base, the task to which Larrabee and her family are now committed.

While, like Long Lance, Marie Lee actively chose to pass, there are interesting moments in the telling of this tale where pheneticization, rather than deliberate racial obfuscation, is a factor. Just as it is difficult to assign a beginning to the moment when Long Lance started passing—was it when he first applied to Carlisle? or when he started calling himself "full-blooded"? or was it by omitting to mention that people back home thought his father was part black?—so it is unclear with Marie. In the film, Larrabee says that when her mother and her aunt arrived in Vancouver's Chinatown as young women, they discovered that they were racially ambiguous in a way they had not been in the rural BC interior. It was the semiotics of context: in Chinatown, Marie's Native appearance could be read as Asian; as a waitress in a Chinese restaurant, all the more so; and, after she married a Chinese man, it was clinched. When people saw her and her husband together, they saw a Chinese couple. And, indeed, it was easier for Marie to be a Chinese wife than it was to be a Qayqayt, married or not. As Larrabee described her mother and aunt's method of passing, it was something they let happen rather than something they forced. "Everyone in town believed that they were Oriental of some kind," says Larrabee in the film. "I think there was some kind of question like, 'Are you Chinese? Are you Hawaiian?' And they would just let people think what they thought. But I think they were happy that they thought they looked Asian of some kind." Later in the documentary Larrabee says, "It was just established that we were a Chinese family," in a grammar that does not name the subject—Marie—as actively passing. Rather, her re-identification is placed in a certain syntactical chain: "it" (her life as a Eurasian Canadian) "was just established"—by Marie herself but by others, too. Marie's youngest

Marie Lee and her daughter Rhonda. Photo: National Film Board of Canada

son, Ron, graciously puts his mother's experience in a social context when he adds in the film, "I don't resent my mother for not being more proud of her heritage. I think she grew up in a very hard time when off-reserve women were treated very badly, if they were Native, by everybody. So, no, I do not blame her at all for that. I know what she must have felt."

Perhaps this is the way with all passing: it begins as possibility. It begins when the phenopolysemic individual is pheneticized in a way that elevates her social status, and she thinks, "Why not?" The phenopolysemic individual, so seen, lets it happen once or twice, then later slides into making it happen, encouraging it, putting some spin on the way her appearance reads and, eventually, at some sticky point, she actively lies to maintain it. If so, this relieves some of the traitorous quality that the term "passing" has acquired. Passing may be treason, but one might also call it entrapment.

The one other place that pheneticization appears in *A Tribe of One* is a scene in which Larrabee notes how, when she was growing up, she mostly believed her mother's story that her origins were just Chinese and French, yet would look at her own face in the mirror, wondering if maybe she was part Native. She would look at Native friends she had in the neighbourhood and wonder if they were somehow her cousins. Larrabee was, it might be said, pheneticizing herself at this young age, reading between the lines of apparent ambiguity and intuiting a seemingly impossible truth.

ASIAN TO WHITE: FRED WAH

If passing always begins with a surprising possibility, a moment in which an individual finds himself pheneticized and decides to let it ride rather than correct the mistake, Fred Wah's book *Diamond Grill* (1996) is filled with examples in which the subject might capitalize on this possibility, but instead does not. His story is not one of someone who deliberately passes at all, but one in which he is repeatedly pheneticized by others, his name often the only thing tripping them up.

Diamond Grill is a collection of short prose-poetic, autobiographical pieces that Wah calls "biotexts"—in which he describes his family's experiences running a series of Chinese restaurants in the twentieth-century Canadian west. Wah is one-quarter Chinese and three-quarters white, having a father who was himself half Chinese and half white. Since Wah's father grew up mostly in Guangdong and was more comfortable speaking Cantonese than English, Wah, though biologically one-quarter, describes an experience in many ways more akin to being half. Wah makes no such claim, but it seems correct in the face of the book's steady accumulation of anecdotes and impressions. His consciousness seems more "inside" particular Chinese moments—most of them centring on food—than his European looks broadcast.

Or do looks ever "broadcast"? Rethinking some of the episodes of Asian-to-white elision in *Diamond Grill* through the concept of pheneticization sharpens the focus on Wah's experiences. In particular, his surname has them guessing, has his interlocutors trying to make their experiences of him match their expectations. He writes, "Sometimes in a store, say, I'm picking up a pair of new kung-fu sandals and the guy checks my Mastercard as I sign and he says Wah! You Chinese? heh heh heh! because he knows I'm not" (1996, 136). Elsewhere he writes, "What I usually get at a counter is the anticipatory pause after I spell out H. Is that it? Double U AY AYCH? I thought it might be *Waugh*. What kind of name is that, *Wah*? Chinese I say. I'm part Chinese. And she says, boy you sure could fool me. You don't look Chinese at all" (169). Another time, his name is Europeanized without the aid of his image: "I had to book a plane ticket over the phone in Montreal and when I went to pick it up I noticed they'd made it out in the name of Fred Roy. The flight attendant even asked if I was related to the Canadiens goal tender, Patrick Roy" (169). The above experiences all take place in Canada. But the experience also occurs when he is overseas: "When I visited China and I told the guide of our tour group that I was Chinese he just laughed at me. I don't blame him. He, for all his racial purity so characteristic of mainland Chinese, was much happier thinking of me as a Canadian, something over there, white, Euro. But not Chinese" (53).

What each of these depictions indicates is an experience in which it is the viewer who acts, not the object viewed. It would be absurd to call these experiences "passing." Wah, the man—or even "Wah," the name—is read, summed up, pheneticized. The cashier "knows"; the clerk Anglicizes; the airline worker Gallicizes; the tour guide laughs. One person actually brings up the idea of deception—that the author "sure could fool" her—because he is a walking prank, an ambush.

Fred Wah. Photo: Charles Earl

The same wording shows up again—of Wah's appearance making a fool out of the pheneticizer—in an incident in which he tries to get a visa to the US:

> (Vancouver, British Columbia, 1963)
>
> Hello is this the US consulate? I'm calling about getting a visa. I'm going to Albuquerque as a graduate student but I'd like to be able to work in the States.
>
> What's your name?
>
> Wah. Double U, Ay, Aych. Fred Wah.
>
> Is that a Chinese name?
>
> Yes it is. Why?
>
> I'm afraid you'll have to apply under the Asian quota, sir, and there's a backup of several years on the Asian list.
>
> But I'm Canadian.
>
> I'm afraid that doesn't matter. If you're of Chinese origin, even if you're born in Canada, you still have to go under the Asian quota.
>
> Well that's ridiculous. Could I come down and talk to the Consul General about this?
>
> By all means, but he's a busy …
>
> I'll be right down.
>
> (fast over to False Creek down Burrard to Georgia—downtown)
>
> And what can I do for you, sir?
>
> My name's Fred Wah. I talked with the receptionist on

the phone this morning about getting a visa. She told me that, even though I'm Canadian, because my racial origin is Chinese, I'll have to apply under the Asian quota.

But you don't look Chinese.

That's because I'm half-Swedish. I'm only quarter-Chinese.

Well, that makes all the difference then. If you're less than fifty per cent you can enter the US as a Canadian. Just ask the girl out front for the forms, it shouldn't take more than a few days. You had me fooled there. (2001, 76–78)

In this case, the experience Wah undergoes is both phenetic and cladistic: ultimately, it is not his appearance that excludes him from the category of Asian, but the state's arbitrary blood-quantum law. Nevertheless, that final statement surely made him wonder how the experience would have gone if, by a different twist of genetics, he *had* looked to the agent more like the agent's expectation of a Chinese phenotype.

As a child, Wah experienced this mix of phenetic and cladistic readings the other way: "When I was in elementary school we had to fill out a form at the beginning of each year. The first couple of years I was really confused. The problem was the blank after Racial Origin. I thought, well, this is Canada, I'll put down Canadian. But the teacher said no, Freddy, you're Chinese, your racial origin is Chinese, that's what your father is. Canadian isn't a racial identity" (1996, 53).

Nevertheless, there are a few moments in the text where Wah

does actively pass. In one experience, he describes disassociating himself from the new Chinese entering his town after the lifting of immigration prohibitions:

> Until 1949 the only Chinese in my life are relatives and old men. Very few Chinese kids my age. After '49, when the Canadian government rescinds its Chinese Exclusion Act, a wave of young Chinese immigrate to Canada. Nelson's Chinese population visibly changes in the early fifties. In a few years there are enough teenage Chinese kids around to not only form an association, the Nelson Chinese Youth Association, but also a basketball team. And they're good, too. Fast, smart. I play on the junior high school team and when the NCYA team comes to play us, I know a lot of the Chinese guys. But my buddies at school call them Chinks and geeks and I feel a little embarrassed and don't talk much with the Chinese kids. I'm white enough to get away with it and that's what I do. (1996, 136)

Wah is honest about how he chooses in that moment to ride the slippage "away"—but that is as active as his transgression ever really gets. His action, in the end, is of bearing witness throughout the whole of the book *Diamond Grill* to the grilling, to the cutting, to the involuntary way he is raced by viewers who are shocked by the trick of his existence.

WHITE TO BLACK: ANTHONY EKUNDAYO LENNON

In 1990 the British Broadcasting Corporation premiered a made-for-television film called *Chilling Out*, which begins with a narration spoken by the actor Lennie James explaining its premise: "All of us in this program are actors, but this is not a fiction. It's come out of real conversations we've had about our lives, which we developed in drama workshops. All of us are speaking as ourselves, and from our own experience. What we've done is draw it all together into an evening over dinner where what we're talking about is the experience and the spirit of being black and living here."

The action starts at the home of one of the actors, Jacqui Gordon-Lawrence, while the group—colleagues familiar with each other, to varying degrees, through the theatre scene in London—gets to know each other better. While they discuss myriad issues—race, class, nationalism, Pan-Africanism, parenthood, and more—I want to focus on a particular actor in this collectively created film: Anthony Lennon, as he was known at the time of filming, now known as Taharka Ekundayo, or by his stage name, Anthony Ekundayo Lennon.

As the opening narration tells us, this film is about "being black" in Britain, and the first few scenes show the actors talking about the differences between black and white cultures, the meaning of the Rasta religion, where each of them is from, and where they have lived. Then they drift into a conversation about Caribbean dialect—how it is maligned by both blacks and whites, and how they are sometimes forced to switch between it and "Standard English." Most of them agree, however, that dialect is something to be proud of. This leads to introductions of the actors' national origins. They go around the room, informally introducing themselves by which Caribbean island their parents are from. Anthony says nothing, until he is asked by Colin McFarlane which island he is from. Comically, he answers, "Ireland," to which Sylvester Williams says, thinking he has misheard him, "Which island?" When Anthony repeats that his parents are from the island of *Ireland*, Jacqui seems puzzled—"Not many black people in Ireland," she says. But a greater shock comes when Anthony explains to them that not only is he not Caribbean, but that he is not black at all—that he is, in fact, white. Sylvester says, in utter shock, "I coulda *swear* you was at least half-caste!" When Anthony tries to "clear this all up" by telling them that his parents—"one born in County Kerry, one born in Tramore"—are both white, adding, "and so are their parents, and so are their parents, and so are their parents," Sylvester interrupts him, saying, "No, man, I don't believe." Anthony starts to get testy and says, "What, you don't believe, like I'm lying or something?" Sylvester is unfazed, and simply replies that, yes, Anthony could be lying. From here, the rest of the actors who did not already know Anthony's background seem stuck on the point. Clare Perkins cannot believe it ("He ain't no white man") and neither can Jacqui ("He looks mixed-race"). In a curious moment, Sylvester examines Anthony's face and notes, "Your eyes are blue as well," as if he is seeing Anthony for the very first time.

Up to this point, the general tone of the discussion is simply bemusement. To them, Anthony looks mixed-race; they have known him for a while now, worked with him in this theatre group in the past, and they have all pheneticized him as having mixed black and white ancestry. And they prefer to believe their eyes over Anthony's own cladistic report of his ancestry. Nevertheless, it dawns on them that what he says may be possible, that he may have some unusual set of features that adds up to a mixed-race appearance.

And so the discussion shifts to something more ontological. Eddie Nestor, picking up on Clare's insistence that "He ain't no white man," asks her "What makes him black?" She answers, "Well, what do you see when you look at him?" to which he can only repeat, "What makes him black?" and to which she can only answer again, slowly and deliberately: "What ... do you see ... when you look at him?" It is as if Anthony is a human tautology; they cannot find a reference point for this turn of events, and can only repeat and circle around inside the insufficient phraseology. Or perhaps Clare is suggesting that if he looks black, he is black—that pheneticization *is* race. But she seems perplexed by her own answer, and later reverses herself. When Eddie finally concedes that he doesn't care, saying to Anthony, "I just see you as black" and "We take you in. We adopt you," Clare complains that he cannot do this, without elaborating on why.

Soon enough, the tenor of the conversation changes from a general discussion of the veracity of Anthony's story and whether or not he is black, to a more accusatory challenge. Sylvester, specifically, angrily brings up the idea that Anthony is

Anthony Ekundayo Lennon. Photo: Joth Shakerley

passing for black—that he is *actively* trying to seem black. "It amazes me!" he spits. "The man speaks in tones and dialects and tongues!" They all briefly discuss Anthony's use of Caribbean dialect—though he only uses it occasionally in the film when singing fragments of various songs. Later, after Anthony discusses his family's unwillingness to talk about race, Sylvester brings up passing once again in an accusatory tone: "Yeah, but you *look* like a black man. Could fool anybody." And, as in the example of Fred Wah, we are back to the idea that the phenopolysemic individual is automatically deceptive and accountable for how others see him. (Anthony's ironic response is to suck his teeth at Sylvester's comment, offering this Caribbean brand of gesture rather than a European shrug.) But Sylvester carries on, clarifying what he means: "Everything about you—your hair, your lips. It's freaky. And I'm telling you, you even *dress* like a black man. Your hat and everything." To this, Anthony admits to what may be an element of passing, saying, "The hat was a conscious decision." But when he goes on to explain, we see that his adoption of a sartorial blackness was prompted by earlier experiences of pheneticization: "When my hair was shorter, it looked like a little Afro, and people just assumed, 'You're half-caste, i'n' it?' And when I was younger, I used to go, 'No,' and try to explain. And after a while I just got sick of it—the explaining, and 'Is he this?' and 'Is he that?' and the scrutinization, and 'You're lying, man!' One day I'm walking through Brixton and there's this man selling hats. I stood there for a second. And I bought one. And since then people don't question it. I mean they see a shape being cut on the street and they just do not question it." Despite this, Anthony asserts, "I'm not walking around to fool."

Their conversation about Anthony's identity seems to finalize at two polarizing issues. First, whatever the facts of his genetic background, it becomes obvious that Anthony has grown up with the experiences of a mixed-race black person. He describes multiple events in which he endured racism growing up and in the present, from being called a "nigger," to having had people throw stones at his mother for "dealing with a black man," to being treated with suspicion by store owners. Second, as an actor, the issue is partly resolved by the simple fact that he "can't get white parts." When he relates these experiences, the other black actors bond with him along the familiar lines that surviving racism can inspire. As Lennie puts it, "Regardless of how Anthony decided to run his life, he would never be able to live his life as a white man, pure and simple."

Nevertheless, the film takes a somewhat ugly turn when, after all the various kinds of racial logic are exhausted, some of the actors—primarily, Lennie—continue to question Anthony's experience. Jacqui asks him, "What colour do you see yourself as?" to which Anthony carefully responds, "Well, when I'm alone in my bedroom looking in the mirror ... thinking about stuff I've written down ... thinking about my past ... relationship-wise ... pictures on the wall—[*Long pause.*]—I think I'm a black man. I've not said that to anyone. And I won't say it outside. I mean—I just won't." His response is telling: to Anthony, the claim to blackness is not frivolous and depends upon not only his physical features or how others read them, but also upon his representation of himself *to himself.* How he deals with people, and how they deal with him, is a large part of it, but also, intriguingly, Anthony believes that *what he writes* reveals himself as black. How he interprets the world as much as how the world interprets him is what determines his race, as far as he is concerned. It is a marvellous sort of self-definition, and it is a non-racial kind of racialization, dependent only upon fluid circumstance.

But the more traditional, and more mystical, form of racialization is the only challenge left to Anthony at this point, and it is taken up by Lennie, who won't let the issue go. After Anthony says that he believes he is black, Lennie retorts, "You can't say that. Just like that." And he later complains privately to Clare that Anthony might have the right to say he's black, but that he might say it "too soon," and he complains that Anthony is slowly acquiring blackness by copying Lennie, which bothers him for some reason he doesn't state.

Clare seems ready to consider Anthony black if she can answer the question of what it is that makes him black—but she has no answer for this. She realizes they are all scrutinizing him, yet she isn't sure what it is they are searching him for. Lennie later gets Anthony alone and voices his complaint: "I am who I am because of my mother and my father and back, and you're not [...] I just want to make sure you're all right underneath it all, underneath the Mandela T-shirt. And when you go see your mum, is it the Mandela T-shirt you wear, or is it some bloody shamrock or something? What language do you dream in, An?" And it is here that the questioning of Anthony's identity seems most cruel, and seems to have gone beyond need. Lennie is asking him to be *metaphysically* black—to embody some undefined essence. The surface is not enough. Neither is experience. After we have boiled it all down to this hermetic logic, the group finally leaves Anthony alone and moves on to other issues, leaving the question open.

What is important about Anthony's experience in this film seems to hinge on this final retreat to an intangible black essence. What it reveals, I think, is that letting Anthony go on as black, when he is, apparently, a man whose black experience exists only in circumstance rather than in some transcendental quantum, exposes *all* racial identification as equally superficial. It makes *every* black person's black experience potentially referenceless and contingent, and this is something the others find difficult to accept in the film. If there is no metaphysical definition of race, as Anthony's Derridian blackness seems to prove, then there is no means to measure or stabilize it. Depending upon your depth of investment in race as a notion, this is either frightening or freeing.

It is interesting to note that today, long after the televising of *Chilling Out*, Lennon continues to work in black theatre in the UK, and he continues to identify as black. On one currently active website, where Lennon is listed as a lecturer, the issue of his ancestry is described as follows:

> Born to Irish immigrants & raised in West London,
> his birth name was Anthony David Lennon although
> his name has changed legally several times over the

years—now, most people know him by his stage name
of Anthony Ekundayo Lennon or his preferred name of
Taharka Ekundayo. It is over a long period of time that
he has delved deeply into a continuing study, re-educa-
tion, appreciation and application of world culture and
wisdom.

From birth, Taharka was viewed by family and society
as a child of "mixed race" heritage: his infant and junior
years were full of incidents of being questioned, positively nurtured or sometimes physically/psychologically
attacked for being a black child in a dominantly and
institutionally racist white society. It was not until a shift
in personal awareness and consciousness during his late
teens that he fully comprehended the circumstances of
his birth in relation to "Race," "Identity" and "Culture."
(*Hogarth Blake*, 2009)

While the wording of this biographical note is a bit vague,
it is also honest—he is Irish, he grew up being thought of as
mixed-race, and, as he indicated in *Chilling Out*, his identification with blackness is, to him, largely a matter of his own path
and perspective.

THE PASSING OF PASSING

At the close of this circle of racial transgressions—making our way around from black through Native, Asian, white, and back to black again—the re-reading of these ostensible "passing narratives," armed with the notion of pheneticization, provides more subtle details of the experiences discerned in each case. Less unfair suspicion is put upon these racialized individuals, and their agency is more apparent in the language describing the events of their lives. What also emerges, interestingly, is the identitarian puzzle at the heart of the contemporary consensus that race is merely a pseudo-science, like a murderous kind of astrology—that, in the matter of race, surface may be all, as we see in Anthony Ekundayo Lennon's case, or nothing, as we read in Fred Wah's stories of being seen and not seen. The wholly social phenomenon of racialization *refers* only to other social phenomena, to the customs of a town like Winston or a city like London, to a surname or a bureaucratic typo, a reductive law or a lazy language, a blaming look or a fear of being fooled. But a *human* is always at the centre, whether his or her features are legible or not. A person who tries to decipher a word that is new to him does not accuse the word of treachery; neither should one do so when an individual's ancestry does not fit the expectations of a particular time, place, or racial reader.

NOTES

1 The established term for this is "hypodescent," the assignation of the racial identity of a mixed-race citizen to the politically repressed group rather than the advantaged group. The antonym is "hyperdescent," the policy of assigning mixed-race people to the dominant group. The US one-drop rule is an example of hypodescent, and the general Latin American convention of excluding mestizos from social classification as Indigenous is an example of hyperdescent.

2 Ultimately, I settled on the term "pheneticizing" here, as opposed to "phenotyping," because of the freight it carries in the history of taxonomy. The problem with using "phenotyping" as the term for what I describe in this essay is that the word is actively used to classify actual species, and I do not want to reinforce the fallacy of race as science. "Pheneticizing," I think, works better because, embedded in the methodological history to which it refers, the term connotes estimation, guesswork, and indeterminacy—and it ultimately failed as a project. It also provides a natural antonym, for my purposes, in the term "cladisticizing," which I repurpose to mean reference to actual ancestry rather than an account of visual cues. Furthermore, while "phenetics" is in use as a noun, "pheneticizing" is not used by biologists in verb form, which should discourage its elision with notions of race as scientifically measurable.

When I corresponded with Dr Mark D. Engstrom, the Senior Curator of Mammals at the Royal Ontario Museum, he generously provided this summary of the history of phenetics and cladistics, which I believe supports my usage as a metaphor for racial reading:

> Phenetic classification was formally proposed by a group of taxonomists known as "numerical" taxonomists. It was developed in reaction against a system of taxonomy that attempted to blend information on overall similarity with information on genealogy to arrive at an overall system of classification (somewhat inappropriately re-

ferred to as evolutionary taxonomy). Blending these two kinds of data leads to a hybrid classification based on evolutionary history and phenetic similarity, which was described as part art and part science. It was classification as subjectively envisioned by the expert taxonomist working on the group and not strictly repeatable by an independent, objective observer—it was taxonomy by authority. Phenetics, on the other hand, had a measurable, repeatable means of determining relationships (overall similarity) based on the premise that two organisms that were most similar would most likely be closely related. For example, a white-tailed deer looks more similar to a mule deer (both in the genus *Odocoileus*) than it does to a moose (genus *Alces*). The taxonomists went on to work on methodologies for determining overall similarity—through measuring as many characters as possible in a large sample of organisms and then creating algorithms to analyze these big data sets, making comparisons of the characters simultaneously. This multivariate approach was only really practical with the advent of computers—and put the "numerical" in numerical taxonomy. Pheneticists believed that the actual evolutionary history of relationships among organisms was in some sense unrecoverable (at least directly), and that overall similarity, using as many characteristics of an organism as possible, provided the best approximation.

Predictably, there was backlash against this point of view, which was vociferously taken up by a group interested in discerning genealogical relationships directly, and then basing classifications on those relationships. This philosophy was called phylogenetic systematics

(or cladistics). It sought to analyze characters in such a
way that evolutionary sequences could be traced in their
transformation. For example, if, in a single family of
beetles, some species had five segments in their antennae,
others had four, and still others had three, you would
look to the nearest known related family of beetles
to see how many segments they have. If they all have
five, by this outgroup analysis, the most likely ancestral
state for this character in the family you are studying
would be five segments, and states three and four are
modified or derived from the ancestral state. By looking
at suites of characters in this way, you can group species
based on patterns of shared derived character states. For
example one group of four genera of our original family
of beetles might all have three segments in the antenna
and be the only ones that have this state, suggesting they
shared a more recent common ancestor with three segments, separate from the other genera in their family. In
phylogenetic analysis you look for this special similarity
of shared derived characteristics, and hopefully corrobo-
rate the pattern with several independent characters that
help you recover the sequence of divergence of species
in evolutionary history (i.e., the branch points on the
evolutionary tree). So the cladists are attempting to recover the actual evolutionary history/branching sequence
of life, which the pheneticists regarded as unachievable
windmill tilting.

The pheneticists and cladists battled it out in the pages
of *Systematic Zoology* and other journals during the
late 1960s and 1970s to the ultimate demise of phenetics as a means to a classification end. Each vehemently

opposed the other camp, agreeing only that they despised the evolutionary taxonomists. Phylogenetic systematics (or cladistic) taxonomy today is the norm and has been greatly aided by a huge new data source—DNA sequencing. I believe we are on the verge of resolving most of the major branches on the evolutionary tree of life—something I could not have conceived of when I was in grad school. This exciting accomplishment is attributable both to new data sets and advances in philosophical/methodological approach. ("Re: 'pheneticizing'?", email to author, April 12, 2010)

For a recent and deeply comprehensive explanation of why race is scientifically invalid as a method of human classification, see Guy P. Harrison, *Race and Reality: What Everyone Should Know About Our Biological Diversity* (Buffalo, NY: Prometheus, 2009).

BLACKVOICE AND STATELY WAYS: ISAAC DICKSON, MIFFLIN GIBBS, AND BLACK BRITISH COLUMBIA'S FIRST TRIALS OF AUTHENTICITY

I don't tink Mr. Editer, dere is a more motly kermoonity in de worl dan dat ob Cariboo, war so mush ob de genwine dust and black san' is 'malgamated an' passes at de same rate ob curncy, yet in dis same little kermoonity war equality is alus sposed to lay on de same rok, an' war no uppa streek effises, deres some foo bright specimens dat tinks deys from de uppa streek, an' dat de sack in which deys 'posited 'tains noting but black san', ob coss alus exceptin' derselves, dey knows eberyting an' is smarter dan de balance. It's to some ob dese bright specimens I's 'bout to say a foo words, an' if de cap I's 'bout to 'facter fits any ob de boys, de bes ting dey can do is to ware it widout saying a word, and den praps nobody but derselves an' dere culed fren' will be any de wiser; at de same time I kermends to dere notis de follerin' words:

"O, wad sum power de gify gib us,
To see us-selbes as udders see us."

—Isaac Dickson, letter to *The Cariboo Sentinel* (Dixie 1865b)[1]

We had no complaint as to business patronage in the State
of California, but there was ever present that spectre of oath
denial and disenfranchisement; the disheartening consciousness that while our existence was tolerated, we were powerless
to appeal to law for the protection of life or property when
assailed. British Columbia offered and gave protection to both,
and equality of political privileges. I cannot describe with what
joy we hailed the opportunity to enjoy that liberty under the
"British Lion" denied us beneath the pinions of the American
Eagle. Three or four hundred colored men from California
and other States, with their families, settled in Victoria, drawn
thither by the two-fold inducement—gold discovery and the
assurance of enjoying impartially the benefits of constitutional
liberty.

—Mifflin Wistar Gibbs, *Shadow and Light: An Autobiography with Reminiscences of the Last and Present Century*
(1995, 63)

Mifflin Wistar Gibbs and Isaac Dickson were businessmen and
sometime writers who lived and worked in British Columbia
in the late nineteenth century. Gibbs had worked in a variety
of fields before arriving in Victoria, BC, from San Francisco
in 1858, including carpentry, boot retail, and newspaper editing. He had also been an abolitionist activist in Philadelphia,
his city of origin, where he had worked closely with Frederick
Douglass. In 1858, at the beginning of the Fraser River Gold
Rush, Gibbs established himself as the proprietor of a general
store in Victoria. Later, Gibbs served as a city councillor and,
for a time, as acting mayor. In 1870, at the age of forty-seven,

he returned to the United States, settling in Little Rock, Arkansas, where he eventually became the first African American to be elected as a municipal judge. Far less is known about Isaac Dickson. He was probably American by birth, like the majority of blacks in BC at the time. He was a barber who owned a shop in Barkerville during the 1860s. There are a few records that give us a suggestion of his life in the Cariboo. But the most spectacular was his role in a jurisdictional struggle along the lawless Fraser River that came to be known, hyperbolically, as McGowan's War. Dickson was assaulted by a white American miner, and his lodging a complaint touched off a dispute between regional magistrates that required the governor to launch a gunboat and a hundred sailors in order to quell the unrest (Hauka 2003, 138–46). Because there is no record of his death in BC, it seems probable that in the 1870s Dickson went back to the country of his birth, along with many of the other blacks who returned after the gold boom had fizzled out and the American Reconstruction offered the hope of a new, more racially equal order in the US.

An educated man born into Philadelphia's black middle-class, Gibbs first wrote in the capacity of a political agitator. He published articles in abolitionist papers and came to edit the first explicitly abolitionist newspaper in San Francisco, *The Mirror of the Times*. In Victoria, as in San Francisco, Gibbs proved himself a reliable and eloquent spokesman for the black community, first by writing letters to *The British Colonist* in response to various racist attacks and provocations against the black community. He also later served as a correspondent to the black-owned San Francisco newspaper *The Elevator*, which was sold as far north as Barkerville.[2] The writing that Gibbs will primarily be remembered for, however, is his memoir, *Shadow and Light: An Autobiography with Reminiscences of the Last and Present Century*, published in 1902. He wrote this book late in life, after his return to the US, but a substantial section of it is devoted to his years in BC.

In contrast to the relatively prolific Gibbs, Isaac Dickson published, in all, merely two short but fascinating letters to the Barkerville newspaper *The Cariboo Sentinel* in June and July of 1865. Whereas Gibbs was a well-known public figure in Victoria and wrote as such, Dickson cultivated a smaller, more local fame in Barkerville. The barber shops, which were monopolized in BC by blacks, doubled as centres for gossip and socializing, and it seems likely that Dickson's two letters to *The Cariboo Sentinel* were an extension of his position as a community character who had assumed a satirical authority to comment on the goings-on of the northern boom town. While Gibbs wrote his letters and later his memoir in the high-toned and Latinate style that was popular in the Victorian era, Dickson wrote his two letters in a phonetically scripted dialect—ostensibly a dialect of the African-American South. His first letter to the editors of *The Cariboo Sentinel*, published in the paper's inaugural issue, predicts that the community's reception of the newspaper should and would influence their mandate: "I dont dout, sar, de paper will 'tain heap dat's headifying and instructin to de miners ob dis country but dont flatter yerself, mister editer, dat de teaching will be all on your side ob de kitchin, an 'emneting from yer own valable resaucers 'tirely, coss if yer does yer slip up on dat air 'rangment you got darn sight to larn from de poplation ob dis garden of 'Lestials, Injuns, white men and culed genelmen an darn sight to see dat'll sprise an' muse yer" (Dixie 1865a). As if to punctuate the origin of this dialect, he signed these letters "Dixie."

The regional and racial milieu in which both Gibbs and Dickson wrote influenced their writing and reception. Examining accounts of whites who lived in Victoria for their impressions of the black population reveals a repeated criticism levelled against the blacks for supposedly speaking and affecting mannerisms above their class and station—and in their divergent ways, both Gibbs and Dickson were writing back to this local prejudice. Sophia Cracroft, the niece of Sir John Franklin, who was travelling through Victoria in 1861, describes in a letter her encounter with two members of Victoria's black community: "Mr. Moses calls himself an Englishman, which of course he is politically & therefore justly. She [Mrs. Moses] is a queer being, wears a long sweeping gown without crinoline—moves slowly & has a sort of stately way (in intention at least) which is quite amusing. Sometimes she ties a coloured handkerchief around her head like the American negroes (she is from Baltimore) [...] The language of both is very good" (in Kilian 2008, 65-66). Cracroft's patronizing description of the husband and wife betrays her expectations at the same time as it denies them; namely, she gives away her belief that Moses is *not* quite an Englishman, that his wife is *not* in fact "stately," and that their language, which she stresses is "very good," is anomalously so. The primary opinion one hears in this description is that these two blacks—refined in appearance and speech—are by the very fact of their blackness merely posing and pretending. Mr Moses *is* an Englishman, but only if we add the proviso "politically"; Mrs Moses *is* stately, but the parentheses are provided as repositories of the unsaid and undercutting racist assumptions—"(in intention at least)."

R.C. Mayne, a commander of the Royal Navy stationed at Esquimalt, also wrote of the black population of Victoria in his memoir, *Four Years in British Columbia and Vancouver Island* (1862). His summary is interesting for its contradictory logic. Mayne despises white Americans for their racism, and presumes a British racial objectivity, but is still annoyed by the presence of a visible black middle-class:[3]

> I must not omit to mention the African Negroes, several hundreds of whom left California when British Columbia sprung into life. It is well known to all who have lived among Northern Americans that they treat free negroes infinitely worse than an Englishman would treat a dog. In California neither coloured men nor Chinese are allowed the benefit of the laws, such as they are, and their evidence is not taken in the courts, so that a black man may be murdered in the midst of a hundred other blacks, and if there is no white man to impeach the murderer, redress cannot be obtained. This feeling was not lessened in the hearts of the Americans at Victoria when they found this hated race, that they had ill used in every way, enjoying precisely the same privileges as themselves.

The consequence was that on one occasion there was a
pitched battle in the theatre between blacks and whites,
in which, I believe, the former came off victorious. Then
the whites objected to the blacks being allowed to go to
the same church with them, and actually appealed to the
Bishop to prevent it. The Bishop was firm in his refusal to
do anything of the kind, but I believe many stayed away
from the church in consequence. One of the dissenting
ministers from Canada was obliged to leave the country
for giving the same refusal. The whites all deserted his
church and went to another who was anti-black, the
negroes were unable to support their champion. As a rule
these free negroes are a very quiet people, a little given
perhaps to over familiarity when any opening for it is
afforded, very fond of dignity, always styling each other
Mr., and addicted to an imposing costume, in the way
of black coats, gold studs and watch-chains, &c.; but
they are a far more steady, sober and thrifty set than the
whites by whom they are so much despised. (1862, 351)

Mayne swings seamlessly from a position of liberal superior-
ity, which white Britons often took when speaking of American
racism, to the idea that the blacks are naturally out of place
in refined society. Like Cracroft, Mayne's scrutiny shows his
racism, and its ultimate implication is that blacks cannot *be*
dignified, but can only *affect* dignity.

Another remarkable example of the social regulation of black
British Columbians through language is an account of a black
man named Willis Bond written of in James W. Pilton's "Negro
Settlement in British Columbia, 1858–1871." A contemporary

of Gibbs and Dickson, Bond owned a public house in Victoria. He was also a self-styled orator who went as far as building a lecture hall as an addition to his bar so that he could sponsor his own debates and lectures on various topics. Working from an incident described in James Robert Anderson's "Notes and Comments on Early Days in British Columbia, Washington, and Oregon" (1925), Pilton writes:

> An amusing anecdote, told by one of Victoria's early citizens, would indicate that Bond was not always too certain about the meaning of the words he used. When James Anderson had refused to buy some manure from the would-be orator, saying that he could get all he needed from over the way for nothing, Bond replied "You don't get nothing for nothing, Mr. Anderson, depend upon it the owner of that manure will circumbent [sic] you, and in the long run you will find yourself defrauded." "You are a pessimist," said Anderson. "No, Sir, I ain't, I ain't," replied Bond. "What was that word Mr. Anderson, I would like to use it in my next speech?" And apparently he did, but with little concern for its proper meaning. (Pilton 1951, 63)

What is remarkable is that an echo of this anecdote appears in a reference to Seraphim Fortes (better known as Joe Fortes), Vancouver's popular first lifeguard, whom the black cultural critic Peter Hudson describes as "the city's first unofficial mascot [...], a coonish, Zwarte Piet-like Jamaican who spent the early part of the twentieth-century saving white kids from drowning in English Bay" (2001). In an article in *The Vancouver Province*, Bruce Ramsey relates this story:

> One of the legends which has grown up around Joe Fortes' memory is that he persuaded the police commission to issue him a uniform, complete with brass buttons. A month later, Joe made his first arrest.
>
> He had warned a couple that their behavior down on the beach was, well, a trifle indiscreet, and when they failed to pay attention to Constable Fortes he hauled them off to jail.
>
> Joe liked to use big words although quite often he didn't know what they meant. He made some up as he went along as well. When the magistrate demanded to know the details of the charge laid against the young couple, he blurted out they had been acting with "agglutinated auspiciousness."
>
> "Case dismissed!" declared the magistrate.
>
> After that, Joe never made another arrest. (1964, 4)

Both of these anecdotes have a minstrel dialogue quality, and, in the second, Ramsey gives no source for the story, telling us only that it is "One of the legends which has grown up around Joe Fortes' memory." Given Cracroft and Mayne's examples of the white expectation of black aphasia, as well as the popular tradition of minstrelsy, which once almost solely prescribed the image North American whites had of blacks, one wonders if these stories had any truth to them at all, or were rather merely generic scripts rehearsed overtop of real-life figures.[4]

This sort of scrutiny was applied specifically to Gibbs himself more than once. Cracroft's entire summary of Gibbs after meeting him was that he was "a most respectable merchant who is rising fast. His manner is exceedingly good, & his way of speaking quite refined. He is not quite black, but his hair is I believe short and crisp" (in Kilian 2008, 65). Here, Cracroft strings together Gibbs' class, speech, and colour in a way that can only suggest that she takes these elements as inter-related; he is middle-class, he speaks well, he is not exactly black. Similarly, a description of a campaign speech Gibbs gave while running for city council, reported in *The British Colonist*, associates his speech with his race, repeating the notion that his language is too elevated. It is useful to look at the description of Gibbs' speech alongside the author's summaries of the other candidates in order to see how he singularly marks Gibbs' race and locution for scrutiny:

> Mr. James Thorne next came forward, and offering himself as a candidate, was well received, and promised, if elected, to look after his own property and that of his fellow-citizens, and watch his brother Councillors.
>
> Mr. W.B. Smith candidly confessed that he was no orator, but pledged himself to act fairly and honorably if elected, and to consult the best interests of the city.
>
> Mifflin W. Gibbs (colored) delivered a long-winded and flowery address, but many portions of it were well

received and, although it had the effect to thin the house, taken all in all, it was a very creditable effort.

Mr. R. Lewis denied that he was a Government candidate, as had been asserted elsewhere; he was in favor of independent and fearless action in the management of municipal affairs.

Mr. John Copland was an independent man from first to last, and would work honestly, wholly and solely for the interests of the town.

Mr. James Carswell was called for, but being absent—

Mr. Wm. Leigh presented himself as candidate, promised to perform his duty faithfully, and declared his belief that in a very short space of time our young Colony would prove a focus from which we should see radiating the rays of a great empire. ("Rise of the Curtain on the Municipal Candidates" 1862, 3)

While the author disdains Gibbs' manner of speech, he concludes his brief description with the same backhanded approval that Cracroft and Mayne exhibit when speaking of those whom they find unexpectedly articulate.

It is true that Gibbs wrote in the high-sounding style that was de rigueur for the Victorian period in which he lived. In *Shadow and Light*, his description of the function of a memoir displays his sententiousness:

For effective purposes one must not be unduly sensitive or overmodest in writing autobiography—for, being the

events and memoirs of his life, written by himself, the
ever-present pronoun "I" dances in such lively atten-
dance and in such profusion on the pages that whatever
pride he may have in the events they chronicle is somewhat abashed at its repetition.

Addison truly says: "There is no passion which steals
into the heart more imperceptible and covers itself under
more disguises than pride." Still, if in such memoirs there
be found landmarks or precept or example that will
smooth the ruggedness of Youth's pathway, the success
of its mission should disarm invidious criticism. For
the merit of history or biography is not alone the events
they chronicle, but the value of the thought they inspire.
(1995, 62)

This style of prose is ubiquitous in the newspapers and
books of the time and can hardly be considered peculiar to
either Gibbs himself or to the blacks of the city of Victoria by
extension. A quote from Reverend Mathew Macfie, a white
Congregationalist missionary who sided *against* the Victoria blacks in their struggle for integrated seating in a local
church, uses the same ostentatious style as Gibbs (including
a fondness for aphorism) in his very denunciation of Victoria's black population: "This preponderance of colour in the
chapel, however, did not accord with the objects the negroes
were ambitious of attaining. They gradually withdrew to the
fashionable church where they could enjoy the satisfaction of
mingling more largely with the superior race; and, like the
ass in the fable, between the two bundles of hay, the devoted

friend of the African was thus starved out. So ungratefully are the disinterested services of philanthropy sometimes requited!" (in Kilian 2008, 48). Gibbs' speech and prose would not have been at all unusual to the ears of his nineteenth-century audience, but rather were typical of the period's public discourse and idiom. In *Shadow and Light*, Gibbs employs throughout what are standard stylistic markers of the Victorian era: Latinate syntax; didacticism; frequent quotation and paraphrasing of authoritative maxims. It is, then, the mere fact of Gibbs' blackness that prompted white objection. Gibbs was speaking and writing in an age still haunted by the racism of the Enlightenment, which posited literacy as a prerequisite of humanity, and, conversely, the absence of letters a sign of subhumanity. As Henry Louis Gates has said, referring to the critical context surrounding the first texts written by blacks in English after 1760, "the production of literature was taken to be the central arena in which persons of African descent could, or could not, establish and redefine their status within the human community. Black people, the evidence suggests, had to represent themselves as 'speaking subjects' before they could even begin to destroy their status as objects, as commodities, within Western culture" (1991, 781). As Gates explains, the political implications of black proficiency in English were what made necessary a letter of authenticity—signed by eighteen of "the most respectable characters in Boston"—which originally prefaced Phillis Wheatley's *Poems* (1773), the first book published by a black North American (783). In Gibbs' time, this interplay between language and status that overdetermined black life persisted. His choice to employ the public discourse as adeptly as possible was surely motivated by a desire to enter a social and political sphere that was in many ways restricted to blacks. The scrutiny and repeated censure of black speech during this time arose out of the desire to maintain and extend those restrictions. A part of this racist strategy of containment was the insistence that black speech that employed public discourse with any level of skill was always little more than coarse imitation.

In seeming contrast to the case of Gibbs, reading Dickson in context actually proves a similar point about the racist reception of black speech and writing in BC. The first scholars to analyze Isaac Dickson's writing—the two main historians of black British Columbia, James W. Pilton and Crawford Kilian—disagree over the "authenticity" of Dickson's language in his two letters to *The Cariboo Sentinel*. Pilton writes that Dickson's letters are "written in the usual phonetic spelling of the almost illiterate negro" (1951, 163); in other words, this Southern dialect is the usual or "authentic" language Cracroft, Mayne, and others expected to hear when conversing with the blacks they encountered in BC. Kilian, however, complicates this analysis, writing that Dickson "had a quick sense of humor, and [...] used dialect to poke fun at life in the gold fields," and that "[i]n our own genteel era, dialect humor has unpleasant overtones of Stepin Fetchit, but a century ago it was an accepted means of mixing laughter and social criticism. Isaac Dickson showed talent in the form" (Kilian 2008, 77–78). In other words, Kilian identifies Dickson's letters as performances of language—as consciously constructed satire—and not merely the extemporaneous out-pourings of a Wordsworthian "natural man."

Indeed it is clear that Dickson's letters show signs of a literacy in both minstrelsy and canonical English literature. In a very short space, he quotes and alludes to Shakespeare's *Macbeth* and *Othello* and, significantly, the Scottish dialect poetry of Robert Burns. The supposed Southern black dialect Dickson uses is played to the hilt, far more excessively than the dialectal phoneticization that appears in slave narratives of the same period. In a line such as, "I hab red shakespuses yarn ob de culed genelman ob Veners dat was tried for 'lopeing wid de owl genelman's darter" (Dixie 1865b), the dissonance between the author's knowledge of Shakespeare and the language in which he spells Shakespeare's name as "shakespuses" can only be read as purposefully inflected irony.

Furthermore, his social commentary in the letters is in places controversial. For example, Dickson writes sarcastically of an upcoming election in which there is a black candidate: "I hope, sar, yer goin to put de bes man in, de culed genelmen de best, but as de 'jority ob de boys is not culed genelmen, best for de country's good to put in de white man, assiss de subjecs, mister editer, ob dis loyel counry to get good resprentives" (Dixie 1865a). And in his second letter, he points to Barkerville's condition, as a gold mining town, as having a less sharply defined class system, and he criticizes those who would try to instate an upper class in the region by referring them to Robert Burns' lyric poem on the same theme, "To a Louse." Dickson's association of himself with Burns, the well-loved Scottish dialect poet, is a wily tactical manoeuvre for legitimizing *black* dialect in a colony where much of the white population was of direct Scottish origin.

But even more than the subject matter of the letters, Dickson's performance of language is itself socially critical. Dickson's readership would have been familiar with the popular minstrel shows of the time and the printed minstrel-inspired dialogues that appeared in newspapers all across North America, including Victoria's *British Colonist*, which reprinted such articles from American papers. The key to the minstrel shows and dialogues was that they were performed by whites in "blackface" for white audiences, using black dialect as the vehicle for and subject of the humour. In a complex gambit, Dickson, as other blacks have done, exploits the presence and popularity of this racist form to produce a more serious commentary. The most well-known example of this black *détournement* of minstrelsy is the music of the Fisk University Jubilee Singers, who toured the world singing slave spirituals, trading largely on the popularity of the comedic minstrel shows which had preceded them, but subverting that comedy and often surprising audiences with the moroseness of the songs they performed. In *The Black Atlantic: Modernity and Double Consciousness*, Paul Gilroy explains how the Fisk Singers' tour of Europe in the early 1870s was the beginning of the internationalization of black popular culture. Gilroy notes that the Fisk Singers were billed as "Negro Minstrelsy in Church" but with "genuine negroes"—an oxymoron, considering that minstrelsy itself was defined by the fact that the performers were whites in "black-face" (1993, 88–89).

The text *Minstrel Gags and End Men's Hand-Book*, published in New York in the nineteenth century, provides a number of what were called "Ethiopian Dialogues," minstrel routines written for performance. The following gag from the dialogue "Bones in Love" by J. Harry Carleton shows the standard format of the performances, in which the Interlocutor converses with the End Man:

> *Interlocutor.* I say, Bones, were you ever in love?
>
> *Bones.* I wasn't nothin' else, old hoss.
>
> *Interlocutor.* What kind of a girl was she?
>
> *Bones.* She was highly polished; yes, indeed. Her fadder was a varnish-maker, and, what's better still, she was devoted to her own sweet Pomp.
>
> *Interlocutor.* What do you mean by that? She must have been a spicy girl.
>
> *Bones.* Yes, dat's de reason she was so fond of me. She was a poickess, too.
>
> *Interlocutor.* A poetess, you mean.
>
> *Bones.* Yes, she used to write verses for de newspapers.
>
> *Interlocutor.* Is that so, Bones?
>
> *Bones.* Yes, saw. De day I went to de house, I—golly!—I dressed myself to kill, and my ole trunk was empty. Well, just as de gal seed me, she cove right in—she was a gone

> coon. When I left, she edged up to me and whispered, "you're too sweet to live." Next day I got a billy-doo.
>
> *Interlocutor.* How do you know it was a billet-doux?
>
> *Bones.* 'Cause Billy Doo was de name of de boy dat brought it. (n.d.)

In the minstrel shows, the Interlocutor stands in as the white subject—the Standard English prosthesis for the ever-white audience. Dickson exploits this accepted form by himself assuming "blackvoice" and beating his audience to the punch(line) by pre-empting the Interlocutor and leaving the white readership at sea, as it were. Without direction as to who or what is the joke, but knowing only that this language must be funny, the white readers of *The Cariboo Sentinel* are made to laugh at themselves—Dickson's letters mock virtually every level of society in the Cariboo—while they believe they are laughing at Dickson's "unsophisticated" language. By bypassing the Interlocutor and donning the language of minstrelsy, Dickson can get away with saying virtually anything, because the white readership is outflanked into thinking that no guile could come from a person using such unpretending grammar.

There is little recorded response to Dickson's letters, apart from a single editorial comment published after his last letter, inviting him to write again, and a later letter written by one Robin Adair which imitates Dickson's, but in Scottish dialect. Adair's letter briefly chastises Dickson, saying that he should take Burns' words "hame to himsel" (1865, 1). It is unknown what Dickson's black readership thought of his letters. Speaking of the black response to the Fisk Singers, Paul Gilroy says that they "encountered the ambivalence and embarrassment of black audiences unsure or uneasy about serious, sacred music being displayed to audiences conditioned by the hateful antics of Zip Coon, Jim Crow, and their odious supporting cast" (1993, 89). It is possible that Dickson's letters received a similarly chilly reception from his black readership in the Cariboo. Perhaps this is why Dickson never published more than these two letters.

Reading Gibbs and Dickson today, it is important to consider them precisely as *writers*, and to remove them from the anthropological gaze that they were subjected to in their own time, and that has subsequently been maintained by critics. The anthropological gaze reads black writing for its representative quality rather than for its capacity to produce conscious, individuated perspectives, and it is the cause of a particular kind of no-win situation: no matter if the black writer produces work in Standard English or black dialect, the writing will be deemed, for different reasons, to be inauthentic; Standard English is considered to be mimicry, while dialect is viewed as failed or "broken" English. Gibbs and Dickson—writing at opposite poles, in totally different styles—were both misread by white audiences whose sightlines were occluded by these racializing myths. What these myths obscure is the fact that *all* writers are inauthentic in the sense that the texts they create are works of artifice, carefully and deliberately contrived. The burden of anthropological representation placed specifically on black authors functions as a means to contain them within expected boundaries. Looking for a representative black language in the work of Gibbs and Dickson is a pursuit that disregards their talent for manipulating language and contexts of reception, which they both did with skill and awareness. What we are left with, if we choose to consider them as agents rather than as passive producers of language, are the beginnings of a tradition of strategic discourse rather than a mythology of essential utterance.

NOTES

1 At the end of this passage, Dickson has "translated" two lines from the poem "To a Louse" (1786) by Robert Burns into a version of black English. Compare with Burns' original lines: "O wad some Pow'r the giftie gie us/To see oursels as others see us!" (1986, 93–94).

2 *The Elevator* was not the only black-edited newspaper from San Francisco read in British Columbia in the nineteenth century. Pilton cites an instance in which a split in voting strategies within the Victoria black community in 1864 was actually argued out in the pages of the San Francisco black newspaper *The Pacific Appeal* (1951, 108). While blacks used BC newspapers for public purposes—such as the debates over segregation in Victoria—it seems that they preferred to use black newspapers from San Francisco to discuss internal community problems. See also Gibbs' "Letters to Bell" published in *The Elevator* on April 25, May 8, June 26, and July 31, 1868, each summarizing the politics and social atmosphere of BC for blacks who were considering emigration (in Pilton 1951, 222–27).

3 It should be mentioned here that a large part of the black population of Victoria was middle-class. Many from San Francisco had been the community's entrepreneurs and small business owners there who could afford the move north.

4 To his credit, and as an example of the inconsistent and unpredictable nature of white attitudes about blacks in BC, Ramsey also penned a very supportive article that speaks of the emigration of blacks from Vancouver to the US as lamentable (1952).

SEVEN ROUTES TO HOGAN'S ALLEY AND VANCOUVER'S BLACK COMMUNITY

1: A HISTORY

Recent books like *The Vancouver Achievement: Urban Planning and Design* (2003) by John Punter and *City Making in Paradise: Nine Decisions That Saved Vancouver* (2007) by Mike Harcourt and Ken Cameron portray Vancouver as a model of global urban development—adding to our local language the self-congratulatory shibboleths "livability," "eco-density," and "Vancouverism." Punter admires Vancouver from afar (the United Kingdom); Harcourt and Cameron present accounts of their own roles in the planning of the city. Both positive appraisals are echoed in the popular imagination, which is phrased by Douglas Coupland in *City of Glass* (2000), where he suggests Vancouver was untouched by the evils of twentieth-century planning regimes: "Many of the factors that stripped the innocence away from other cities never occurred here: freeways were never built and a soul-free edge city never arose" (34).

None of these narratives mentions Vancouver's black community, many members of which, during the mid-twentieth

century, lived in and around Hogan's Alley, a sub-neighbour-
hood in the East End/Strathcona area that was destroyed by
the construction of the Georgia and Dunsmuir viaducts, the
completed first steps of a larger freeway plan that was ultimately stopped. Vancouver's black community suffered what
their American cousins, punning on the term "urban renewal," called "Negro removal"—the destruction of the politically weakest community of a city for large modernist planning
schemes. The viaducts were part of an urban revision that had
evolved out of earlier "slum clearance" endeavours. The collapse of the plan in the late 1960s—after its scope, formulated
in secret by the city council, was revealed and subsequently
fought against by local residents—brought down a right-wing
civic party monopoly that had lasted for nearly three decades.
Nevertheless, the destruction of the black community that was
at the centre of these upheavals is rarely mentioned. Vancouver's planning successes in the 1970s and into the present are
usually related as though no community paid a price for them
to happen. But by tracing the history of these events all the way
to their roots, it becomes apparent that—despite Harcourt's
assertion that the city was "saved"—from the perspective of
the black community, this part of the city was shamelessly sac-
rificed. It was a scapegoat of the union between an authoritarian planning ideology and a developer-led civic government.

While Greater Vancouver has been home to original peoples
such as the Stó:lō, Musqueam, and Squamish for over 10,000
years, its beginnings as a colonial civic project lie in the late
nineteenth century when white settlers began to exploit local

resources at sites such as Moodyville and Hastings Mill. A small number of black people participated in these proto-civic projects. Among the first black Vancouverites was the Sullivan family—Josephine, who "ran a small restaurant in Gastown," and her husband, Philip, who ran a general store and "was the village's leading musician" (Macdonald 1992, 21); their son Arthur continued the family business in the nascent city site at Granville (Kilian 2008, 134). The Sullivan name appears on the documents of incorporation for the city of Vancouver in 1886 (Macdonald 1992, 21). And Deas Island on the Fraser River between Delta and Richmond is named after John Sullivan Deas, another famous early black Vancouverite, who established a successful salmon cannery in the 1870s (Kilian 2008, 130–31).

Most of the blacks in nineteenth-century British Columbia arrived as part of a self-directed group migration from San Francisco to Victoria, coming at once over the course of the spring and summer of 1858 after choosing the site at a series of church meetings. The two instigating factors were the Fraser River Gold Rush and, more importantly, the increasingly hostile Californian racial climate as it edged from territory status toward statehood, initiating an official Jim Crow segregation as it went along. The blacks who arrived in Victoria established vibrant communities there and on Salt Spring Island, and smaller numbers of them spread as far north as Barkerville and beyond. But after the North won the American Civil War, the black population of BC shrank as many returned to the US to participate in the Reconstruction. Further black migration

Fielding William Spotts outside his home at 217½ Hogan's Alley. Spotts was born in the US and brought to BC by his parents as an infant in 1860. He was raised on Salt Spring Island and in Saanich. When he was a young man, he moved to Vancouver, where he died in 1937, the year after these photographs were taken. These images are among the very few extant pictures of black residents of Hogan's Alley *in situ*. Photo: City of Vancouver Archives, Port N3.1

to the province after this period became, as Kevin C. Griffin puts it in *Vancouver's Many Faces* (1993), "episodic" (24)— that is, individually motivated.

As the centre of economic power in BC moved from Victoria and New Westminster to Vancouver, blacks from all parts of the province moved there (along with other British Columbians), seeking jobs. Some blacks also came from the US and the Caribbean and from other parts of Canada. In Canada, as in the US, the railways preferred to hire black men as porters for passenger cars, creating a job ghetto there. Whereas in the US this lubricated an internal diaspora that ran south to north, in Canada there was an east-west population transfer; black men working as porters from cities such as Halifax, Montreal, Toronto, Winnipeg, and Edmonton travelled regularly to the western railway terminus at Vancouver, where they sometimes had to layover awaiting the next job eastward again.[1] Indeed, one of the earliest sites of black presence in Vancouver's East End was the Pullman Porter Club, operated, according to the city directory, by O.K. Rooks from 1927 to 1928 at 804 Main Street. The address is noted as featuring "billiards," so one imagines a lounge where these men could spend the hours between jobs socializing without concern about racial restriction. The club backed onto a T-shaped alley whose north-south spur was called "Park Lane" and whose east-west path was colloquially known as "Hogan's Alley."

In a document titled *Vancouver Redevelopment Study*, published internally by the City of Vancouver Planning Department in 1957, the anonymous author counts the presence of

Hogan's Alley, 1958. Photo: City of Vancouver Archives, Bu P508.53, A.L.
Yates

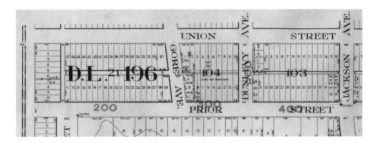

Area Surrounding Hogan's Alley, 1939. Photo: City of Vancouver Archives,
Location 268, Drawer 5, Item 7 (9)

the porters as one of three reasons explaining the localization of the black community in the East End/Strathcona[2] (of which Hogan's Alley was one small part): "The Negro population [of Strathcona], while numerically small, is probably a large proportion of the total Negro population in Vancouver. Their choice of this area is partly its proximity to the railroads where many of them are employed, partly its cheapness and partly the fact that it is traditionally the home of many non-white groups" (49). Furthermore, Leonard C. Marsh wrote, by way of explaining the black presence there, that "There is a small colony of Negro families, numerous enough to represent nearly 3 per cent of the total [of Strathcona's population]. Many of them could afford to live elsewhere, but it is too obvious that they would be unwelcome" (1950, 8), adding a third reason for this quasi-segregation: that while First Nations people and Asians were officially segregated in Vancouver, no such laws prohibited blacks. Marsh instead notes a general ad hoc racism that contributed to the advent of the East End/Strathcona as a black residential space.

In 1923, a group of local black Christians bought the Norwegian Lutheran Church at 823 Jackson Avenue and established the Fountain Chapel, an African Methodist Episcopal (AME) church, flanking onto Hogan's Alley. Nora Hendrix, the paternal grandmother of the musician Jimi Hendrix, was one of these early black Vancouverites who helped to found the church by raising funds that were matched by the AME administration in the US (N. Hendrix 1979, 59). Pastors were brought up from the US to minister at the church in its early decades. The Fountain Chapel occupied that space, sometimes under different names, but with some continuity, until 1989, when it was finally sold to the Basel Hakka Lutheran Church. It was decommissioned by the Chinese Lutherans in 2008,[3] and is currently a private residence.

While, as mentioned, many of the black male residents were porters, the community's first business owners were women. Rosa Pryor, "Mother" Alexander, Vie Moore, and others established a series of what came to be called "chicken houses," restaurants that sometimes also doubled as speakeasies. The most successful of these belonged to Moore, a descendant of the black pioneers of the 1850s. Vie's Chicken and Steak House operated at 209 Union Street from 1948 to 1980, at the northern end of Park Lane.

In 1929, Harland Bartholomew & Associates published *A Plan for the City of Vancouver*, a report commissioned by the city council. While the intention of the report was to rationalize Vancouver's layout after it was amalgamated with South Vancouver and Point Grey, for Hogan's Alley this was an early salvo in a series of plans hostile to its residents. The Bartholomew Plan led to a 1931 bylaw zoning much of Hogan's Alley and its surrounding area as industrial rather than residential. John Atkin describes the effect this bylaw wrought, in his book *Strathcona: Vancouver's First Neighbourhood*: "Homeowners felt the effects of the plan immediately, when they found that lending institutions didn't consider a home in an industrial district to be a good risk. Money for mortgages and home improvements was virtually unobtainable. Real estate

agents were more interested in selling lots for industrial redevelopment than for continued home ownership" (1994, 59–61).

By 1939, newspaper articles had begun to represent the
neighbourhood as a problem spot. In April of that year, the
Vancouver Province ran four articles about Hogan's Alley, all
sparked by a report issued by an assize jury of the BC Supreme
Court on slums, which had been issued in the previous month.
Helena Gutteridge, the first woman elected to Vancouver's city
council, answered this report by launching a social housing
campaign (Wade 1994, 90). Her goals were progressive and her
methods were ahead of their time. She advocated pressuring
slum landlords to renovate and improve the housing already
there or else face clearance rather than the wholesale razing of
neighbourhoods (Howard 1992, 201–02), and she met with
women's groups and locals as part of her process (*Vancouver Daily Province* 1939, 6). Nevertheless, Gutteridge lost the
1939 civic election and the campaign died with her removal
from the council and the start of World War II. Furthermore,
despite Gutteridge's sympathetic intervention, the newspaper
articles covering her efforts use a poor-bashing phraseology,
showing a biased disdain for Hogan's Alley, and focusing on
its abject status. For example, in "Hogan's Alley Fate at Stake,"
journalist Jack Stepler introduces his subject by writing, "To
the average citizen, Hogan's Alley stands for three things—
squalor, immorality and crime," and he goes on to describe
some of the neighbourhood's most sensational and gory mur-
ders (1939, 29). The presence there of honest labourers, small
business owners, families, and a church community that would

last for more than six decades was swept aside in this sort of crime-obsessed journalism.

It is also worth noting that the appellation "Hogan's Alley," as applied to this part of the East End/Strathcona, first appeared in print with the publication of these 1930s *Vancouver Province* articles. While Elizabeth Walker, in *Street Names of Vancouver* (1999), links the informal title to an early resident named Harry Hogan (56), Tom Snyders and Jennifer O'Rourke are probably closer to the truth when they cite the Richard Outcault cartoon called *Hogan's Alley* (Snyders and O'Rourke 2002, 134), which appeared in *Truth* and the *New York World* from 1894–96. Therein, Outcault depicted a fictional New York ghetto he called Hogan's Alley in one-panel drawings that showed frenzied and crowded scenes of urban squalor. Outcault's satire was directed primarily at Irish immigrants, who were at that time a racialized target of Anglo-Americans, but it is easy to see how this popular comic title may have been used as a synonym for any poor and neglected North American neighbourhood with an immigrant population. Indeed another BC town—Rossland, in the interior near the Canada–US border—called its red-light district "Hogan's Alley" as well during this same period.[4]

While Gutteridge's campaign failed to make Hogan's Alley a rallying point for the establishment of social housing, with the publication of Leonard Marsh's *Rebuilding a Neighbourhood* in 1950, another attempt at social housing in the area was launched—one which did not believe in pressuring landlords or consulting residents about what they wanted done to improve their living conditions, but which believed in sweeping changes to the cityscape as the answer. Marsh was a professor in the University of British Columbia's School of Social Work and was, like Gutteridge, a democratic socialist. (His most famous achievement was providing the report that became the basis of Canada's social security policy.) But unlike Gutteridge, Marsh's direction for the East End—which he renamed "Strathcona" (1950, 2)—was akin to other early architects of the emerging continent-wide movement called "urban renewal." Marsh's ideas were more like those of Le Corbusier and Richard Moses, the city planners of Paris and New York, who favoured the car over public transit as well as uniform high rises over mixed-use dwellings and the conservation of historical buildings. The urban planning example set by Moses in New York sparked American and Canadian interest in top-down city restructuring, with a heavy focus on freeway creation and slum clearance.[5] This ideology went hand-in-glove with oil and automobile interests, as well as old-fashioned racism: freeways were invariably run through black neighbourhoods or Chinatowns, poor districts whose populations were least able to lobby civic governments. Curiously, while Marsh's inspiration for such large-scale, government-led urban planning was socialist in origin—he was a president of the Fabian-like League for Social Reconstruction—there seems little practical difference between the Marsh plan and similar corporate- or state-driven projects elsewhere. Nevertheless, planners of varied political stripes rationalized their actions during this period by declaring that these neighbourhoods were, in the language of the day, "blighted," and therefore in need of clearance (Marsh 1950, 2; Atkin 1994, 73). Old neighbourhoods, which had arisen organically over several decades, were flattened, uniform tower-block "housing projects" were erected, and the displaced residents were shifted into them. Initially touted as achievements of rational planning, these projects quickly became worse than the initial "slums" had been, particularly in US cities. Where the previous neighbourhoods had had social networks and community-created methods of coping with poverty, the apartment projects were alienating. These bleak tower blocks resisted improvement and renovation and became vertices of urban despair rather than utopian answers to poverty. And while the former neighbourhoods were poor, residents who managed to ascend in class through hard work or luck sometimes stayed and bought property there, creating communities that were a mix of social classes. The high-rise projects, however, were places from which economically successful residents fled, leaving behind an increasingly underclass population in their wake.

In Vancouver, Marsh's report was ultimately taken up by the right-wing, business-vectored Non-Partisan Association (NPA), which ruled the city council throughout the middle decades of the twentieth century. The NPA developed the plan together with the University of British Columbia in secrecy, perhaps aware that, were their intentions made explicit, there would have been a community backlash. Atkin notes that "a show was made about consultation with the residents" in 1957 in the form of a misleading letter from the mayor implying that improvements would be made to the neighbourhood, but with "no mention made of the fact that the city had already decided that complete demolition of the neighbourhood was the only improvement necessary" (1994, 74). (The NPA also colluded with developers, who added a waterfront commercial complex called Project 200 to the plan—a freeway running through Hogan's Alley and Chinatown that would connect to it from Clark Drive and First Avenue, with the Trans-Canada Highway as its source. Later, it was hoped, this freeway would go on through a tunnel that was to run beneath Burrard Inlet, creating a third crossing to North Vancouver.) Following the logic of the 1931 zoning bylaw into the 1950s, the NPA ceased granting building and development permits in the area and stopped funding improvements to roads. Eventually they froze property values in Strathcona altogether, discouraging any improvements by local owners (Atkin 1994, 60, 75). Although the freeway plan itself was not announced, to anyone living in the East End/Strathcona during these years it was clear that the neighbourhood was not favoured and was facing, at least, a turn to heavy industry and, at worst, a radical revision or total demolition.

When the NPA finally revealed the plan in 1967, it did indeed create popular outrage in the neighbourhood. An organization calling itself the Strathcona Property Owners and Tenants Association (SPOTA) was quickly formed to counter the project. Local figures like Mary Chan were instrumental in the opposition, and Mike Harcourt began his foray into politics as the movement's lawyer.[6] Still, because they had done all

Construction of the Georgia Viaduct on top of the old Hogan's Alley site,
November, 1970. Photo: City of Vancouver Archives, CVA 447-374, Walter
Edwin Frost

their preparations in secret, the city council was able to quickly
launch their mission while the opposition was still coming together. In the process, the western end of Hogan's Alley was
assessed for expropriation, property owners were summarily
compensated by the city, several blocks of houses were demol-
ished—including the sites where the old porters' dormitory had
been, as well as the residence of Vie Moore—and the building
of the first phase of the freeway—the viaducts—was begun in
1967 and completed in 1971.[7] The next step in the plan was
to lay the eight-lane freeway overtop the rest of Hogan's Alley,
but, as Punter writes in *The Vancouver Achievement*, support
for the scheme evaporated quickly when it was exposed to public scrutiny: "When these clandestine plans were presented in
June 1967 to council as 'the Vancouver transportation study,'

angry citizens convened public meetings citywide. [...] When it became clear that the proposals were being steered by such powerful landholders as the National Harbours Board, Canadian Pacific, and BC Hydro—all enhancing their own development interests—even development supporters such as the Downtown Business Association and the Vancouver Board of Trade began to question city planning and development practices. In the end, only the Vancouver Planning Commission supported the freeway proposals" (2003, 24). Punter goes on to explain how the commission chair was compelled to resign after a show of public opposition at open meetings in the fall of 1967. And so, finally, the entire project was scrapped due to its obvious unpopularity, leaving only the viaducts as a vestige of the failed plan (24).

In an infamous incident, Vancouver's mayor at the time, Tom Campbell, a long-time NPA member who had won as an independent when the party declined to endorse him, blamed the failure of the plan on "Maoists, Communists, pinkies, left wingers, and hamburgers"—the latter was his personal term for people who did not have university degrees (in Punter 2003, 24). But Campbell and the NPA's hubris failed them, finally, in the 1972 civic election where they were defeated by The Electors Action Movement (TEAM)—a slate that arose largely in response to the unpopular scheme. Out of these struggles, a viable leftist challenge finally emerged in Vancouver's civic politics in the form of the Coalition of Progressive Electors (COPE), a socialist and social democratic slate, which eventually went on to back Harcourt's win as an independent mayor in the

1980 election. (Harcourt would also later lead the New Democratic Party to provincial victory in 1991.) Thus the "achievement" Punter describes, and the "saving" of Vancouver in Harcourt's telling, really mark this late turning point rather than the whole of the history—which includes the complex fate of the black community.

At the moment that the NPA revealed the freeway plan in 1967, the black community had largely already left Hogan's Alley and Strathcona. Personal anecdotes, the membership of SPOTA (mostly Chinese), and examination of the city directories seems to bear this out. But while the census material counting Vancouver's black population is sporadic for the first half of the city's existence, both the Marsh report and a later city report (mentioned above) observe that a large part of the city's black population lived in Strathcona until the 1950s; and oral histories confirm that Hogan's Alley was a specific site of black residence, business, and church life.[8] But it is important to note that Hogan's Alley was not at all an exclusively black neighbourhood: it was also home to Italians, Asians, First Nations people, and others. It seems most correct to say that Hogan's Alley had a black community within it, and one that was conspicuous enough that some do refer to the neighbourhood itself as a racially black-identified space. If we consider it a fair estimate that the area had a sizeable black population at least as early as the 1923 establishment of the Fountain Chapel, but had ceased to be a constellating site for black Vancouverites by 1967, then the question is when and why did the black community in general leave?

Rev. J. Ivan Moore welcomes Mrs. Robert Crump, her twin sons Robert and Ronald, 12, well-known Vancouver entertainers, and Sandra, 5, to Fountain Chapel.

When Foote's Loose I

1952 *Vancouver Sun* article on the black community. The photograph features the Crump family ascending the steps of the Fountain Chapel at Jackson Avenue. Photo: *Vancouver Sun*

While no census numbers were taken in the 1940s because of the war, in 1950, Marsh puts the "Negro" population of all of Strathcona at 2.8 percent of the total, while seven years later the City Planning Department puts it at three percent. Marsh's survey takes account of a thirty-one-block area, whereas Hogan's Alley was about three or four blocks long, depending on how one counts it. If those blacks were concentrated in or even near that small an area, it would be correct to call it a black neighbourhood. Marsh may suggest this when he writes in 1950 that, "[t]here is a small *colony* of Negro families" (8; my emphasis) in Strathcona, probably referring to the Hogan's Alley site, though he does not name it. The *Vancouver Redevelopment Study* refers to different ethnic enclaves within Strathcona, but also does not name the zones: "The disruption of accustomed social arrangements, which is an inevitable concomitant of relocation, is bound to create special problems for these minority groups. It is, therefore, important that the relocation programme should be flexible enough to allow members of the same ethnic group *to remain* together while at the same time discouraging the formation of ethnic enclaves" (1957, 49; my emphasis). The study's authors, in other words, noted groupings of different minorities in Strathcona in 1957, and were conflicted about disrupting them. As Dorothy Nealy, a one-time black resident of Strathcona who was interviewed in the 1970s said, "When I came here, this district was Negroes, from Main Street to Campbell Avenue, like you see the Chinese here now. Whole apartment blocks that were all full of Blacks. In '44 it was a ghetto" (1979, 169). So reading between the lines, this suggests that Hogan's Alley had its black community through the twenties, thirties, and forties, up to at least 1957. And then, in the next decade, the community left. Since there is no record of another black locus in Greater Vancouver thereafter, it would seem that this was the moment that the black community integrated with the general population of the city—a condition that stands today. The questions remaining are, why did they leave, and why did they not set up another enclave elsewhere?

Backing up a little, the Marsh plan, apart from its end result, was a very close reflection of the US urban renewal strategies that were executed throughout the 1950s: a black community was marked for clearance; housing projects were built for the displaced to live in instead; and a freeway was constructed where the old neighbourhood once stood. In most US cities, the next part of the pattern followed simply—the black population moved into the projects. The only unforeseen deviation was that the more upwardly mobile of these blacks split off to form black middle-class enclaves elsewhere or integrated with the general population. But in Vancouver, the pattern deviated more significantly. The black community was indeed targeted for clearance; housing projects were indeed built for the displaced to live in—the MacLean Park project was completed in 1966 just a block over from Hogan's Alley and the Raymur Social Housing Project was built in 1970 a little farther east in Strathcona,[9] but only a segment of the freeway was built before it was aborted, and the black community did not move into the projects that were made for them—instead they left Strathcona altogether, integrating and ending their condition of pseudo-segregation for good.

Why things happened this way in Vancouver, and why there was a departure from the American trend, is yet to be discerned. I would forward three possible reasons. First, the black community of British Columbia, going back to the first arrivals in Victoria during the Gold Rush, has always been ardently integrationist. Indeed, before the black migrants from San Francisco came in the summer of 1858, they explicitly planned to stick to a political course of pro-integration rather than developing parallel black institutions. It was believed that, in British territory and under British law, integration would be possible in a way that it was not in the US. The black population of Victoria underwent two highly publicized and heated integrationist struggles, at a church and at a theatre, in the 1850s and '60s.[10] Although the black population of Vancouver in the early to middle twentieth century was not completely descended from this earlier BC black community, it does seem possible that the political tendency asserting that equal rights would come through social integration survived and prevailed among Vancouver's blacks, and met its eventual success in this period.

A second possible reason for a different pattern of urban renewal in Vancouver may have been the particular way that the advent of the Civil Rights era altered the racial climate in Vancouver. In the wake of the vast social changes that were happening across North America in the 1960s, black Vancouverites may have taken this opportunity to re-test the will of white landlords in other neighbourhoods, and discovered that new doors were open to them. If one counts the beginning of the US Civil Rights movement in 1955, at the start of the Montgomery, Alabama bus boycott, then this seems plausible. The anti-racist consciousness raised by these US events may have both emboldened Vancouver's blacks and eroded the racism of its whites, and thus led the way out of pseudo-segregation in Hogan's Alley at the very end of the 1950s through the early years of the 1960s.

A third reason is suggested if one imagines that the number of blacks in the 1950s already showed a decline, and that the peak of the population was at some point earlier, perhaps in the 1940s. If the black community had already decreased by the time Marsh and his group of University of British Columbia students started going door-to-door to count them, it might suggest a cause rooted in the peculiar racial order of Vancouver as opposed to most other North American cities: that is, though black Vancouverites suffered every disadvantage that their American cousins experienced—poverty, racism, the legacy of slavery—British Columbian racism and racist policy has traditionally been directed at the demographically larger minorities, specifically First Nations people and people of Asian descent. So perhaps events such as the repealing of the *Chinese Exclusion Act* in 1947 focused racist feeling away from the black community as the Chinese population of Vancouver grew. It is altogether plausible to look at Vancouver as a kind of inverse of US racial trends, a place where racist whites most feared Asians rather than blacks, and blacks rather than Asians took the place of the so-called "model minority." If this is true, then black Vancouverites may have sidestepped the fate of their inner-city American cousins more because of local demographics than continent-wide trends.

And, of course, it is possible that the process of integration came through a combination of these factors: the discouragement caused by urban renewal policies; the proactive integrationism of Vancouver's black community; the US Civil Rights movement; and the idiosyncratic way anti-*black* racism was offset by anti-*Asian* racism in Vancouver.

Whatever the case, after the fall of the NPA in 1972, while a few blacks continued to live in Strathcona (including Nora Hendrix, Dorothy Nealy, Leona Risby, Rosa Pryor, and Austin Philips, interviewed in the late 1970s by Daphne Marlatt and Carole Itter in *Opening Doors: Vancouver's East End*), and, as mentioned, the Fountain Chapel and Vie's Chicken and Steak House survived into the 1980s as exceptionally long-lived community institutions, by 1990 there was nothing left that would remind one that there had ever been a black community in Strathcona at all. Greater Vancouver today has a population of 20,670 blacks[11] who occupy the city at large, and hold no substantive claim to Strathcona apart from memories, photographs, a record of newspaper articles, and a body of interviews, art, and creative literature. Hogan's Alley, like its American counterparts, did indeed suffer "Negro removal"— but without moving to approximations of the post-renewal housing projects that have become infamous there, but rather through a course of complete integration.

2: A HOME

A history is one way to narrate the story of Hogan's Alley. But I realize that the one I've written above leans heavily toward demographics, planning, and the institutional racism that influenced Vancouver's black lives in the last century. A social history would look different. A subjective account of the place, and why it matters to me and to others, might start with the fact that those numbers—the 20,670 blacks who live here now—so often get minimized out of existence when people comment on the demographics of Vancouver. There are no black people in Vancouver, people often say. Twenty thousand-plus out of two million may indeed be a small percentage. But it is more than nothing. The perceived absence of blacks in Vancouver is a sort of optical illusion: black people today represent a higher percentage of the total population than they did fifty or a hundred years ago, yet it seems like Vancouverites are less aware that blacks live here today than they were then. A scattering, an integration, partly forced, partly wanted, has made for no place, no site, no centres residential or commercial, no set of streets vilified or tourist-friendly, and no provincial or federal riding that a politician would see as black enough to ever rate the wooing of a community vote. Twenty thousand-plus people are here and there—somehow unseen. This is a good place to begin an explanation of the current generation's interest in Hogan's Alley—a subjective exploration of how and why the history matters.

Hogan's Alley is not a significant site in my own family history. None of my relatives has ever lived in the East End/Strathcona. But my mother and father did meet for the first time somewhere near Hogan's Alley in the 1950s, when they and their friends enjoyed the archipelago of nightclubs and speak-easies that once stretched up Main Street. Those clubs, and the Vancouver of my mom and dad's memory, contained a lot of black people. I noticed this when I was a child listening to their stories, but only as an adult did I come to learn of the history of the place and the reasons why there were black people there back then, but very few around in my time. I was born in 1972, and have always known the area as merely the eastern edge of Chinatown, which is what it had gradually become by the late 1960s.

In a city like Vancouver, where there is an absence of a *place* that black people can regularly find each other, Black History Month has become instead a *time* to do so—at various sites, with varying focuses, and open to everyone. Every February, the debate crops up again as to whether or not Black History Month continues to be relevant, and usually you can find someone, black or otherwise, who suggests that it's racist, or ghettoizing, or obsolete. But these debates miss the point. Our "black" families are mostly mixed here,[12] and these events are multicultural. And they are temporary zones in which the community can see itself, can conceive of itself as a "community," can chart its political progress, and can consider the issues specific to it. The value is in the ritual and the regularity; it is not imposed from above, and it is certainly no threat to integration, which is here to stay. So I ardently defend the institution as one of Vancouver's only means of keeping this voluntary connection going. In light of this, it is interesting to note that I first learned about Hogan's Alley, in depth and apart from family anecdote, at one of these events in the 1990s where a key documentary film by Andrea Fatona and Cornelia Wyngaarden was featured: *Hogan's Alley* (1994) presents the oral histories of Pearl Brown, Leah Curtis, and Thelma Gibson Townes, all one-time residents of the East End/Strathcona during the Hogan's Alley era, and describes the neighbourhood in detail. The film is a staple of Black History Month events in and around Vancouver, and serves, I think, as a memorial in motion, one that renews itself every time it is shown. Black History Month, as a concept, answers the Middle Passage and a North American racism that once actively suppressed black history; the thirst for knowledge of a history that was all but severed from the previous generations has passed on to the present one. We return, again and again, to the past to figure out our future. Recovering local black history is no different from the greater, global, diasporic urge. We seek to ease the anxiety of disruption and erasure. In Vancouver, the phenomenon fits together with the city's history of misconceived urban renewal and civic development.

In 2002, I participated in the establishment of the Hogan's Alley Memorial Project (HAMP), a group that came together to think of ways that the black history of Vancouver might be officially remembered. Membership in the group has fluctuated over the years, and it has always been small, but HAMP goes on and is currently active. The first meeting came out of a conversation I had with Sheilagh Cahill, a founding member who, after reading some of the interviews from *Opening Doors* that I had reprinted in an anthology,[13] met with me to talk about them. I can't remember which of us said it first, but we agreed that there ought to at least be a plaque somewhere down there at the site of Vancouver's once-and-only black centre. We gathered together friends who were interested in the place and the history, and we started down a path of information-gathering, exhibitions, informal archiving, interviewing, blogging, and consciousness-raising about the history. There is no plaque there yet, as I write this, but we have not exhausted all channels. Considering the past eight years, I have come to think that, like Black History Month, the temporary sites of memorialization that we have set up, at community and cultural centres,[14] at conferences and as keynote speeches[15]—these seem more important than a plaque might finally be. Speaking face-to-face with people, meeting folks and explaining to them that there was a history, and having them see the way we are drawn to the memory and turn it over and over in our mouths, speaking it alive again in these settings—all this is the ritual of memory, the extension of the lives that were lived through a black ancestry in *that* and *this* place. We remember in the present tense.

I sometimes find my own circumstances strange; that I, a person who has more white than black biological ancestry, have devoted so much of my time to the project of recovering blackness in this place. And also that the segregation that my forebears so soundly eschewed has become, in some ways, a point of crucial interest for my generation; that we seek empowerment there, in a location that they sometimes remember as a place they *escaped* from—a slum or, more gently, the humble origin out of which they happily ascended. More than once in the process of talking to elders, I have been told that I was lucky not to have grown up there. Which is at once a warning to our generation not to romanticize it and, I think, an indirect wonderment of their own: why, they seem to be saying, do our grandchildren and their friends—mixed, integrated, educated—care about this old alley so much, this place that seems to have been the least of our achievements? Getting out, getting our children through school, buying a house, earning a pension, getting a degree, living where we damn well pleased—*these* are the things worth valorizing. This is what I hear sometimes between the lines of their polite answers and generous recollections about that old alley. It is hard to explain to them my own interest, my generation's interest. I can only say that their childhood is now our history; their chicken houses and church and dormitory, as ordinary as they may seem to them, are what we have to look to for a foundational narrative of presence. Even if they were born in Canada, the elders of Hogan's Alley and that generation often look to America, where most of their families were from, to its forms, to its music and heroes, maybe because they were from a time closer to the initial northward migrations; we, the younger ones, feel less American, and look to them and their little community in the East End/Strathcona as something that grounds us in Canada. We need Hogan's Alley because Motown songs and Martin Luther King are from another, different place. They come through the TV. They come through books. Hogan's

Alley, however, ran between this and that side of *right here*.

Perhaps there's a simpler explanation, found in moments of clarity that make the world make more sense. Such as the day I meet with a friend whose father and uncle grew up in the East End/Strathcona during the 1940s and '50s, who were members of the Fountain Chapel congregation. She offers to let me see her family photos. We look through the ancient black-and-white snapshots with serrated edges, photos of finely dressed black men and women in Alberta fixing to leave for the coast during the Depression. The pictures she keeps passing to me out of a set of albums gradually become more and more contemporary; colour photos appear in the early 1960s, showing the blue Coast Mountains behind this black and white family's faces as they frame themselves in our city. I am looking at these photos thinking of history—thinking of the unfolding of a population, and thinking, as I always do, of these family photos as the archive of black Vancouver, the fragile and un-housed and seemingly soon-to-be-lost document of how long we have been here. Our tale, our home. And then, thumbing through the decades into the 1970s, I see a photo of a girl about four years old with a baby on her lap, two mulattoes, and my host says, "This is us." At first I think she is speaking abstractly, ethnically, because that is how I am looking at these pictures: all these photos are us, yes, our shared history. But she points at the photo and says, "You must be about six months old here. This was at my mom and dad's house." And I suddenly see myself in the photo. It is the two of us, and that's my mom at the right, almost cut off by the frame, a photo I've

Left to right: The author, Brenda Crump, and Patricia Compton, Vancouver, 1972. Photo courtesy of Wayde Compton.

never seen before, never knew existed. It's in some other part of East Vancouver, not Hogan's Alley, but in the house of a family who had just moved from there. I too am archival, if not archived; I'm in this project of drawing a line from what was then to what is now. I am in an afterimage of our history.

3: A POEM

In my second book of poems, *Performance Bond* (2004), I included a long poem titled "Rune," which is about the memory of Hogan's Alley, and specifically, the problem of how to remember Hogan's Alley. For me, the *how* of it does not refer to the content of our memories, but rather to the process of remembering: in what ways can and should a person or a community or a city recall such a place?

The poem deals with the ambivalences of looking back, and the enduring curiosity about those times and conditions. I approached this issue from a few angles. In places, I write in the voice of fictional characters who lived in those times; elsewhere the speaker is displaced by time and looks backward. I composed fantastical dialogues, one between two modes of recording technology, Analogue and Digital, personified in screenplay form like the abstract virtues of a morality play; and the last words of the poem belong to a dialogue between a contemporary speaker and a homeless ghost. I wanted to approach the problem of remembering Hogan's Alley not through realistic representation but through more elliptical means. I was less interested, for that project, in what it was actually like then, than in the *desire* to remember.

Toward this end, I imagined elements of the history that never were: a newspaper article of my own creation that appears in the book as if it were photocopied rather than fabricated; staged photographs of four imaginary black East End institutions; and interview transcriptions with fictional subjects who founded two of these institutions. Each of these semi-hoaxes is based on an actual corollary. The newspaper article is based on a story in the *Vancouver Province* by Jack Stepler.[16] The imaginary institutions have real-life counterparts: I imagined a union that is based on the Brotherhood of Sleeping Car Porters, which really did have Vancouver members; I imagined a newspaper that was like a version of the actual *Afro News* that began in the 1980s in Vancouver—my paper was created by imaginary Universal Negro Improvement Association (UNIA) members in a Vancouver that actually did have a small Garveyite presence.[17] I made up a fictitious mosque, counterposed to the real Fountain Chapel, and I placed there a black "benevolent society" akin to the Chinese benevolent association houses that have always been in the East End/Strathcona. Two of the fictional texts mimic the transcribed interviews in Marlatt and Itter's *Opening Doors*; I credit my two manufactured interviews—with two African-American cousins who immigrated to the city in the 1930s—to a non-existent book I dubbed *Portals: East Vancouver Oral Histories*, listed as published in 1972, the year I was born.

The spark of inspiration for this retro-speculative project was a conversation I had with the writer and activist Joy Russell while we were working together in the early days of the

HAMP. I said to her one day that it depressed me to walk through what had once been Hogan's Alley and find absolutely nothing that indicated that a black community had ever lived there, and she asked me, "What do you wish you'd found there?" I had no immediate answer for her, and the question haunted me. I wanted to answer her question in some way, but I also wanted to capture the experience of owning such inchoate desires—wanting something, some mark, some lasting vestige—but what? I wanted to illustrate how the black experience in BC can feel absurd, a place where the founding governor of our colony was one-quarter black, and yet few people know it. A place where the under-visibility of black people belies the fact that there are more blacks in BC than in Nova Scotia,[18] a place where Canada rightly perceives, to some degree, the contributions and presence of blacks. What does one do, in the wake of this kind of history, with the desire not for re-segregation, but for basic acknowledgment?

In his essay "Natural Histories of Southwestern British Columbia," Peter Hudson, exasperated by how poorly our history has been kept, describes a similar response to the lacuna of black presence in local archives: "Even the scant archives the city has on people of African descent in Vancouver seem forged. Often indexed without dates or the names of the journals in which they originally appeared, the records seem to be created by medieval artisans equally satisfied with selling their fake icons as with knowing that people are basing their beliefs on faith alone, ignorant of the veracity of their fetishes" (1997–98, 20–21). Earlier in the same essay, Hudson describes how

he and I used to joke about forging an Afrocentric British Columbia history, echoing the partisan historiographies of mav-
erick writers such as J.A. Rogers, Cheikh Anta Diop, and their
lesser imitators. Russell's question recalled to me these conversations with Hudson, which were essentially about disillusion-
ment with Afrocentrism. I saw that the only way to answer
her would be to create the images of my own latent romantic
pseudo-black-nationalist desires. By making this desired past
"real," I would perhaps complicate and understand the yearning for it. Further inspiration for the photographs of the "Lost-
Found Landmarks of Black Vancouver" in *Performance Bond*
came from visual artist Melinda Mollineaux's "Cadboro Bay
Photographs,"[19] a series she produced while living in Victoria,
and which she describes in an artist statement: "Examining
the colonial histories of Canada's West Coast black settlers, I
discovered that from the time of their 1858 arrival from California, these early immigrants held Emancipation Day picnics
every August 1 at Cadboro Bay in remembrance of the West
Indian abolition of slavery. The Cadboro Bay picnics represent,
for me, a diasporic social space that challenges established
narratives of Victoria's British colonial history. I use pinhole
photography to say, like the picnics, that despite our apparent
invisibility, our experience of life in migration occurs within
a sense of place" (1999, 47). Mollineaux's photographs are
important because they perceptually Africanize a British Columbian space that, similar to Hogan's Alley, bears no contemporary sign of that former presence. But of even greater
significance to me is her use of pinhole photography, a technol-

ogy that could have been available to the nineteenth-century settlers themselves. Mollineaux's choice in using the era's productive means does not merely represent the beach as a sign of that lost past, but creates images that appear as photographs that the settlers themselves might have taken, but never did. In the "Cadboro Bay Photographs," I see a familiar yearning for what the ancestors might have left us and a gesture toward a retro-speculative examination of their endeavours.

To create my four imagined institutions, I enlisted the help of the visual artist Mykol Knighton, who designed and made four hand-painted wooden signs. I found buildings that suggested to me these imaginary sites in and near Hogan's Alley, and I bought some industrial-strength double-sided tape to hang them. I asked the writer and photographer Robert Sherrin to shoot these staged photographs, and the two of us went out to turn the four sites into an alternate image of a surviving Afro-Vancouver. There was some tricky fence-climbing, and we encountered one resident who, when we tried to explain what we were doing to his garage, asked if we were working for a film company; so that he didn't get the wrong idea about the depth of our pockets, we assured him that it was poetry we were making, and he allowed us to get on with it, slightly bemused. The photographs are printed in the middle of the poem "Rune" and are, along with the prose passages that resemble transcriptions of interviews, edited in monologue form. The photographic section is, as far as I am concerned, a poetic device.

While the "Lost-Found Landmarks of Black Vancouver" evoke the issues I intended to explore—namely, the twin senses of displacement and self-enculturation that worry blacks in western Canada—I was initially anxious about the creation of "fake" images of a community in the midst of a difficult process of "real" memorialization. I am aware that, although the book's acknowledgments name the non-historical elements within "Rune," those merely skimming the book or not reading closely, including a majority of readers who will be undoubtedly insubstantially aware of Hogan's Alley or will be hearing about it for the first time, may read the "Landmarks" as actual. My intention is not to hoax such readers, but rather to at once allegorize the ontological feelings emanating from the social and historical conditions I have described above, and to experiment formally with cultural memorialization as a representational act.

One of my hopes is that readers will experience the sensation of acquiring the knowledge of a particular history and then will subsequently feel that history disappear from them with the realization that it is fiction—a process of reading that imitates the conditions of the history itself, the sense of incredulity that our city seems to associate with its improbable black populace.

4: A PLOT

Hogan's Alley Welcomes You
200 block Union St., Vancouver, July 2007
Floral Text (*Impatiens*)

On the morning of Sunday July 8, 2007, a long stretch of
floral graffiti appeared on the green space below the Georgia
Viaduct at the corner of Main St. and Union St. A team of
workers, known as the Vancouver Flower Brigade (VFB)
and captained by the artist Lauren Marsden, planted over
2,000 red impatiens to spell out the phrase, "Hogan's Alley
Welcomes You."

The text serves to beautify the neighbourhood which has
been subject to an onslaught of redevelopment and construction. It also commemorates the former site of Hogan's Alley
which was the first and last neighbourhood with a substantial concentrated black population. The flowers are situated
exactly where the alley used to be. Most of Hogan's Alley
was destroyed circa 1970 by the City Council's construction
of the Georgia Viaduct and it now exists only on the periphery of public memory.

—"Hogan's Alley Welcomes You," Lauren Marsden[20]

The civic powers write—sometimes in floral text—messages
welcoming you into the municipality. But what about the
unofficial spaces? Those that were not named by the city but
named themselves? The municipalities within municipalities?
The lost 'hoods? The ghost ways?

This July, if you're in the vicinity of the green space near the

Georgia Viaduct, at 200-block Union Street—the old site of
Hogan's Alley—check out Lauren Marsden's installation,
lovingly planted with support from HAMP and friends.

—"Guerrilla art and public memory," Hogan's Alley
Memorial Project, weblog entry[21]

View of floral text from the roof of Solheim Place (251 Union
Street), Vancouver. Photo: Lauren Marsden

Visual artist Lauren Marsden (fourth from right), HAMP member
Karina Vernon (second from right), and other Vancouver Flower
Brigade members execute their floricultural direct action. Photo: Wayde
Compton

HAMP members Naomi Moyer and Karina Vernon and other VFB
members. Photo: Wayde Compton

The author planting the "E" in "ALLEY." Photo: Wayde Compton

Preparing the ground for the floral text. Photo: Wayde Compton

5: A TRACT

It is worth considering what *should* have happened to Hogan's Alley had the plans for its demise not been carried out during the NPA years of the mid-twentieth century, in order to better understand that injustice in its time, but also to seek lessons that might be applied to current urban politics. It is remarkable that the contemptuous newspaper articles about Hogan's Alley in the 1930s so closely echo present-day editorializing about Vancouver's impoverished Downtown Eastside (DTES). (From the *Province* in 1939: "It is not possible, of course, to make an area devoted to junk, and the homes of people who make a living from junk, neat and sweet as milady's boudoir" ["Vancouver's Slums," 4]. From the *Province* in 2009: "But the question is always asked when someone looks at Main and Hastings: 'If you clean it up, where will all these lost, drug-addicted souls and all those unpleasant criminals go?' The answer is the same as what happened in New York, and the answer is a question: Where were all those wasted souls before New York hit the skids and before Main and Hastings got to be Shame and Wastings? The answer: they did not exist" [McCardell 2009].) Today the issue has as its focus the illegal drug trade in addition to poverty, but otherwise little has fundamentally changed. Those in power seem just as unwilling or unable today as they were then to improve material conditions in the East End. There is still an inadequate amount of social housing there.[22] Developers and corporations still dictate social policy in the city.[23] And civic governments still rise and fall over issues related to the area: just as the NPA fell in the 1970s, so did it fall in 2002, largely over the issue of what to do about the DTES.[24] But while it is easy to put the blame on the NPA and the logic of developer-led capitalism—which looks at city-planning mainly as a means of enriching large-scale property owners—the history is complicated by the presence of Leonard Marsh and Helena Gutteridge—Co-operative Commonwealth Federation (CCF) socialists—at the centre of the storm that eventually sold-out Hogan's Alley. While, as previously mentioned, Gutteridge was closer to the ground than Marsh, working more directly with local residents and citizen groups, the vague call for "social housing" became, in Marsh's vision, the unilateral government-guided plan to erase and redraw the neighbourhood, a plan that was easily adapted for the NPA's business base, who lobbied to bring freeway traffic to the commercial Project 200. Both the right-wing and the democratic socialist left were capable of the sort of authoritarian urban renewal, tinged with institutionalized racism, that literally steamrolled over the wishes of the renting, working class. So, leaving aside simple ideological formulae, what would have been best for the residents themselves?

We could start with the better instincts of Helena Gutteridge and her social housing campaign of the 1930s, which might have plausibly led to something reasonably fair without restoring to utopian dreaming. Imagine that she achieved two goals denied to her in reality—if she had received the one percent tax needed to fund social housing across Vancouver that she requested (*Vancouver Daily Province* 1939, 6), and if she'd stayed in office through the war years rather than losing her seat in 1939. If a model of urban renewal as a "building pro-gramme to relieve overcrowding rather than slum clearance" (quoted in Wade 1994, 87), rather than community-razing, had been initiated, then affordable housing could have been built in the East End, and this would have required the coun-cil to reverse its industrial rezoning of the neighbourhood in 1931. As a consequence of throwing out that bylaw (and the early Bartholomew Plan), in addition to new affordable hous-ing paid for by that tax, basic improvements to houses already existing in the East End would also have been legal during the war years and onward: streets, curbs, and buildings could have been renovated rather than left neglected for decades due to zoning. There would have developed in the East End (which also probably would not have been renamed) a mix of gov-ernment-built social housing (freeholds or apartments, but no large-scale, alienating projects) and privately owned accom-modations. The freeway—which Vancouver has gotten along without—would never have been promoted. What we would have had instead was a community that retained its organic beginnings as a working-class, immigrant neighbourhood with a continuity that the urban renewal plan broke. It is probable that, while some upwardly mobile citizens might have moved out of the area when their income levels rose—for example, during the postwar boom years and in the later twentieth cen-tury—some whose economic fortunes improved would never-theless have stayed in the East End. More families who started their lives in the neighbourhood as renters would have bought within the neighbourhood when they could afford to do so.

Therefore, more of the old small family businesses begun in the 1940s, like Vie's, would have lasted into the 1980s and later. Without the pernicious urban renewal plan, we would have had what Jane Jacobs describes in *The Death and Life of Great American Cities* (1961) as an "unslumming slum." In her formula for the improvement of a neighbourhood, against the "slum shifting" of urban renewal, is the retention of citizens who otherwise tend to "move out of it too fast—and in the meantime dream of getting out" (271)—which was exactly the case of Hogan's Alley after it was marked for destruction. Using New York as her primary model, Jacobs describes the very same phenomenon that destroyed Hogan's Alley when she writes:

> Conventional planning approaches to slums and slum
> dwellers are thoroughly paternalistic. The trouble with
> paternalists is that they want to make impossibly pro-
> found changes, and they choose impossibly superficial
> means for doing so. To overcome slums, we must regard
> slum dwellers as people capable of understanding and
> acting upon their own self-interests, which they certainly
> are. We need to discern, respect and build upon the
> forces for regeneration that exist in slums themselves,
> and that demonstrably work in real cities. This is far
> from trying to patronize people into a better life, and it is
> far from what is done today. (271)

Jacobs asserts that the corrective for slum conditions lies in the communities themselves, which need "encouragement rather than destruction" (1961, 271). She points out that, "the people who do stay in an unslumming slum, and improve their lot within the neighbourhood [...] seem to think that their neighbourhood is unique and irreplaceable in all the world, and remarkably valuable in spite of its shortcomings. In this way they are correct, for the multitude of relationships and public characters that make up an animated city street neighbourhood are always unique, intricate and have the value of the unreproducible original" (279). It is also important to note that Jacobs' model is different from gentrification in that it advocates the public funding of improvements that benefit the class already living there, rather than the encouragement of upscale development that will ultimately price out locals. Both Jacobs' criticism of paternalism and her notion of long-time residents especially valuing a potentially unslumming slum is echoed by Dorothy Nealy's statements about the implementation of the Marsh Plan and its impact. In an interview, Nealy says,

> When we heard of city council's plans for the neighbourhood, we were horrified, we just screamed. They intended to put high-rises all over here, like the West End. But the people that lived here, we just took up a petition. We got thousands and thousands of names. And we stopped them. The Vancouver Resources Board met with city council and they met with different organizations. They met with SPOTA. You see, it wasn't just SPOTA that fought for this East End. There was the churches and all kinds of people got involved. The whole neighbourhood got involved. Because *we* were satisfied with our neigh-

bourhood. But the people from outside came in, and told us we shouldn't have these houses, we should live in housing projects, we should live in high-rises. But what was wrong with living here? *They* didn't live here, I don't know what they were so worried about. As I said, I've lived here for thirty-three years. I wouldn't want to live anyplace else. But somebody comes over from Dunbar district, looking down their nose at this end of town. It's just like the Christians going to Africa, trying to convert you to Christianity when you already have your own tribal laws and religions and everything else. And that was their attitude when they came down here.

They interviewed every individual and they had all kinds of books. And they'd go from room to room. First thing they'd ask, "Wouldn't you like to move out of here?" We'd say, "Move where?" "Well, out of this neighbour-hood." No, nobody wanted to move out of here. It was just like a village, just the same. You went out the back door, you stood on the back verandah, and somebody'd wave at you, over there. Even if you didn't know them, you'd wave back. And when you walked down the street, you nodded your head. Sometimes you said, "Hello," or you just nodded your head and smiled and kept going. That's the way we lived. (1979, 173–74)

Without the hostile NPA and the Marsh Plan, it is easy to imagine Hogan's Alley as one of Jacobs' unslumming slums from the 1950s forward, and it is easy to imagine the black community maintaining a presence there as part of an improv-ing, multi-class neighbourhood. For the black community, a situation of pseudo-segregation would have transformed into one of a community no longer pressed together by poverty and racism, but one carrying forward a vibrant and continuous civic culture.

But what of this pseudo-segregation and its end? Occasionally, when HAMP has given presentations and talks about Hogan's Alley and has advocated for an organized memorialization of the black community, we have been asked if, since urban renewal in the East End/Strathcona seems to have led to black integration in Vancouver, it might have been, on the whole, a good thing. Sometimes this sentiment is expressed more forcefully, and it is assumed that because we wish to memorialize the historical black community we are pro-segregation or somehow wish for a reversal of black integration. I believe that this response evinces a subtle racism, a stereotypical fear of black organization in any form as threatening or excessively angry. (I have never heard anyone suggest that non-racialized memorials—the Iron Workers' Memorial Bridge, say—are automatic evidence of a desire to return to the social order of those times.) If total integration has been good for the black community in Vancouver, it is nevertheless important to remember the history of pseudo-segregation; and if the black community has landed on its feet, it is *despite* urban renewal and certainly does not justify the authoritarian mishandling of the neighbourhood.

Thinking of Jacobs' notion of the unslumming slum, had Hogan's Alley been encouraged to go that route, I think the black community's presence in the East End would have looked less

and less like pseudo-segregation as the years went by. It ultimately might have resembled something akin to a black version
of Little Italy, as seen on Vancouver's Commercial Drive, an
ethnic presence as part of a historical continuity rather than an
enclave; a porous, multicultural community with a peppering
of black institutions and businesses, and some public acknowledgment of the site as black-identified. Even in the heyday of
Hogan's Alley, the area held only a share of Vancouver's whole
black community; had it been allowed to unslum, it might have
retained a little less of that residential presence, but would have
underwent nothing like the near-total evacuation that actually
happened. Having a continuous and voluntary presence in an
unslummed Hogan's Alley almost certainly would have given
Vancouver's black community a higher social and political pro-
file, with no negative consequences that I can see.

Leaving aside alternate visions of the past, there was, of
course, resistance to the way things actually unfolded. After
the 1952 killing of Clarence Clemons, a black longshoreman
beaten to death in Strathcona by two white policemen, the Negro Citizens League was formed to counter anti-black racism
in Vancouver.[25] The British Columbia Association for the Advancement of Coloured People was formed in 1958.[26] I previously mentioned SPOTA, which put a stop to the later stages
of the freeway plan. But even after the urban renewal plan was
cancelled, in one of the projects that had been built to "slum
shift" local residents, activism emerged in the form of the Militant Mothers of Raymur—women living in the Raymur Social Housing Project (another of Marsh's tower blocks) who

—Glenn Baglo Photo

MILITANT MOTHERS ... all-night vigil kept by lamplight

Raymur Place mothers back on the rails

The militant mothers of Raymur Place staged another great train holdup Tuesday by pitching a tent and mounting an all-night guard along the Pender crossing tracks.

The events were the most dramatic in a series of actions — including demonstrations and a march into city hall last January — which the mothers have staged to win their battle for an overpass.

Some 400 school children cross the tracks daily at the Pender and Raymur Streets crossing.

Until an overpass is built the mothers are demanding that the Canadian National Railways stop using the tracks when children are going to and returning from school.

"We're here and we're not going to budge an inch until our three demands are met," said Judy Stainsby, spokesman for about 40 women who huddled around outside the kerosene lamp-lit tent Tuesday night.

The group charged earlier that the CNR ran a train through the crossing at 8:32 a.m. Monday breaking an earlier promise not to use the tracks at that time.

That particular train, they said, "sped down the track."

A CNR spokesman denied the charge, saying it moved over the crossing at 8:27 a.m. doing no more than six miles per hour.

"We told the CNR if they broke their promise we'd be back on the tracks and now we're here we're not budging until our demands are met," said Mrs. Stainsby.

The three demands are that the Canadian Transport Commission release funds for its share of the cost of an overpass; that the city acquire title to the road allowance where the overpass will be built; and that CNR post a $50,000 bond to keep the terms of the Jan. 6 agreement that trains would be kept off the tracks during certain hours.

"The CNR has lied to us twice," said Carolyn Jerome, a member of the group and mother of two children.

"It's not an extreme step to camp on their tracks when they are running trains through at 35 mph. If this was Kerrisdale, they would have acted quicker."

Dorothy Cox said that she can see the crossing from her apartment nearby.

"I've got two children and every day I find myself watching the crossing and wondering whether a child has to be killed before something is done."

As the group milled around in the mud and intermittent rain, Earl Matheson, CNR superintendent of terminals, arrived.

He told the group that the Canadian Transport Commission had authorized construction of the overpass and would fund 80 per cent of the costs.

"Earlier today (Tuesday) the Vancouver city council approved the purchase and expropriation of property necessary for the overpass," he said.

Matheson said the city had agreed to pay 15 per cent of the costs and Burlington Northern Railway would pay the remaining five per cent.

"What more can be done? The overpass is going to be built. It can't be done immediately. Now are you going to get off the tracks?"

The group said they would not.

"We want proof of everything you have said," said Mrs. Stainsby. "We are talking about children's lives and we're not fooling around with them. When you give us proof we will move."

Matheson said there were three CNR trains in each direction whose passage was blocked and one Burlington Northern train.

"Whatever action will be taken now is up to the vice-president or a senior company official," he said.

But the militant mothers had drifted back to their tent to take turns throughout the night standing guard.

A CNR spokesman said the company will take no action until another attempt is made today to talk to the mothers, who are still blocking the tracks.

Legal action, he said, would be taken only as a last resort.

"There is no logical reason for them to block the track. It is causing serious delays in moving grain for the waterfront. It cannot continue and we hope they will come to their senses," he said.

He said a dozen trains a day normally use the track, most of them carrying grain.

INDUSTRIAL RELATIONS BILL

Article about the Militant Mothers of Raymur from the *Vancouver Sun*, March 24, 1971. Photo: Glenn Baglo/*Vancouver Sun* waged campaigns for neighbourhood safety and the creation of a community centre. For three months in 1971, the Militant Mothers put up sporadic blockades of the railway tracks that run through Strathcona, until the city finally gave in to their demand to build a pedestrian overpass above the tracks so that children didn't have to dodge trains to get to their nearby elementary school. (One of their slogans summed up the issue of social housing in Vancouver concisely: "Children vs. Profit.")[27] One can link this direct action to more recent responses to top-down urban planning, such as the occupation of the Woodwards Building in Vancouver's Downtown Eastside for three full months in 2002 by organized squatters demanding housing for the poor.[28] In the face of seventy years of civic regimes that have consistently put corporate profit before human need, confrontational actions like these, past and present, are justified and inspiring.

6: A COLLAPSE

Discover a collection of concrete, loft-style residences in the heart of Vancouver's original neighbourhood, Strathcona. Look east to V6A and you will find an exciting area experiencing both renewal and transformation. Located just a few minutes from the downtown core, Yaletown, South East False Creek, Gastown and Commercial Drive, V6A is a short bike ride, drive or walk from wherever you need to go. Stake your claim in Vancouver's most up-and-coming urban environment. The time is right to make your move. Don't wait until it's too late.

—Advertisement copy for a high-rise condominium being developed at the old site of Hogan's Alley in 2008[29]

A major developer in Metro Vancouver is being investigated
by an arm of the provincial government after CTV found it
was still selling condos even though construction has been
halted at the project.

It's a big name developer, which has been building in Metro
Vancouver for decades.

On Thursday, the Onni Group of Companies which is
behind the V6A condo complex near Main and Union streets
in Vancouver said the project has been postponed. But when
CTV went to the sales center we discovered the units were
still being offered for pre-sale—and prospective buyers were
not being told the project was on hold.

Now B.C.'s Superintendent of Real Estate is investigating.

—CTV British Columbia website news article[30]

I won't lie—I am whooping for joy. I've seen so many people
sleeping in doorways and bus shelters in that exact same
area, exposed to the elements and other dangers. Single
women, as well. To hell with pricey condos when the homeless are on their own.

—Blog comment about the V6A development crisis[31]

While many experts have suggested that the worst of the
2008 economic crisis is over (as of 2010), the shockwaves of
this global recession, instigated by the US housing market bubble, nevertheless continue to play out. As for the economics,
a cottage industry has arisen to explain exactly why and how

the bottom fell out: books, blogs, radio shows, and all manner of punditry have appeared to auger the mysteries of voodoo economics. We are told it was the ascendance of Third World capital; we are told it was the credit-default-swap system; we are told it was Alan Greenspan's fetishization of Ayn Rand; we are told it was predatory lending.

But in the end it means that money is and always has been *language*, that the political economy is made of what is *said*— and the wealth they said was there was not. Money didn't stop flowing—the idea that we call money stopped flowing, moving, transferring, finding its level. It is a naturalizing metaphor, suggesting that wealth is more or less like weather: it shifts, it flows, it cycles through the biosphere. And the nightmare of capitalists is that all this liquid will freeze in the form of mere words: you *say* this square of earth is worth this much, so it *is* worth this much. But then suddenly nothing is worth anything at all.

The lesson of the collapse, surely, is that this always has been and always will be capitalism's way. It curves toward failure, again and again, though the powers that be seem capable of rebooting it again and again, if we let them. And the other great collapse of our time, of the Soviet Union and its sphere in 1989–91, surely plays a part in contributing to the free-market hubris of our present era. Set up as a straw man, the USSR, as a reference, fuels the "There is no alternative" mantra of neo-liberalism and neoconservatism.

What is certain is that the global contest between right and left ideologies has exerted an influence throughout the history of a few blocks of inner-city Vancouver. The destruction of Hogan's Alley was brought about by the NPA, a civic party formed in the 1930s to unify business-oriented opposition to the rise of democratic socialism in the west. Ironically, the NPA employed a democratic socialist planner, Leonard Marsh, to sketch out its plans for the neighbourhood. While there were better visions of socialism, which sought the answers to community problems by empowering community members themselves (as advocated in Helena Gutteridge's campaign), both sides of the political spectrum were prone to racism and classist paternalism. The lesson for our time—in which global pressures persist to exert authoritarian influence on our poorest neighbourhoods, either through the state or through the tacit rules of developer speculation—is that an alternative to capitalism must be sought, and that it must be an alternative that directly empowers the poor at the neighbourhood level. Anything else will be a continued manipulation of the local sphere by distant, exploitive interests, under whatever political and economic nomenclature.

7: A CODA

Perhaps the best way to perceive the experience of black people in Vancouver is obliquely. Examining the headlines of articles about blacks and/or Hogan's Alley and its surrounding area from both of the city's major newspapers, the *Province* and the *Vancouver Sun*, history, like a figure in a pointillist painting, comes together when seen at a distance:

1900   "Colored Folks in Garments Gay—Observe Emancipation Day"

1927   "Men of Color Formed BC's First Volunteer Soldiers"

1935   "BC's Colored Colony"

1935   "Negroes in Canada"

1935   "Victoria Had Negro Troops 85 Years Ago"

1936   "When Black Troops Volunteered Too Much"

1937   "Slums in Vancouver"

1938   "Hopes To End Slums in Vancouver"

1939   "Grand Jury's Criticism of Slum Areas Wins Praise of Alderman Gutteridge"

1939   "Vancouver's Slums"

1940   "Local Slums a Disgrace"

1941   "First BC Defense Force"

1942   "Is It Hypocrisy?"

1943   "Negroes Subject to Army Call Here"

1944   "Survey Asked of Slum Conditions"

1944   "Life Too Easy Here, Says Negro Pastor"

1944   "Plea for Negroes"

1945   "Hotels Refuse To Take Negroes"

1945   "Carmen Jones' Cast"

1945   "Race Antagonism"

1945   "Negro Ban Story Said Untrue"

1945   "Slum Clearing Cost Shared"

1945   "Slums Breed Delinquency"

1946   "Government's Plan To Eliminate 'Shack Towns'"

1946   "Colored Races May Quit, US Negro Warns"

1946   "Education, Not Politics Answer to Negro Problem"

1946   "Government Takes Control of 'Shack Towns'"

1947   "Sordid, Squalid Slums Black Mark Against Vancouver's Beauty as a City"

1947   "Project May Mean End of Chinatown"

1947   "Negro Band Leader Scores Growth in Race Prejudice"

1947   "Negro Band Leader Barred From Hotel Here"

1947   "Speaker Praises Negro Race"

1947   "Etheopian [*sic*] Student at UBC Scores Racial Prejudice"

1947   "Negro Play Here as Social Protest"

1947   "Our Town"

1948   "Young Negro Couple Threatened With Death Unless They
        Move"

1948   "'Jim Crowism' Feared Here as Warning Letter Received"

1948   "Neighbours Rally Behind Threatened Negro Couple"

1948   "Ku Klux Klan Mentality Is Threat to Local Negroes, Says
        Minister"

1948   "Negro Threat Notes Laid to Neighbour"

1948   "Woman Guilty of 'Jim Crow' Threat Here"

1948   "Arts Flourish at Negro Workshop"

1948   "Unions Hit Pub for Barring Negro"

1948   "Negro Raps Color Bar in Industry"

1949   "Few Occupations Open to Negroes, Group Told"

1951   "BC's Negro Army"

1951   "Police Strengthen Skidroad Patrol; Second Recent Death Murder,
        Report Jury"

1952   "Nicknamed 'African Rifles', Black Troops BC's First Reserves"

1952   "Black Troops BC's First Reserves"

1952   "Negro Company Claimed Pioneer Force of Province"

1952   "Prosecutor Probes Beating of Negro"

1952   "Evidence Lacking in Alleged Beating"

1952   "Vancouver's Shame, Skid Road"

1952   "Clarence Clemons Dies in Hospital"

1953   "Tragedy on the Skid Road"

1953   "Caldwell Visits Our Skid Road"

1954   "Vancouver Island School Ousts Jamaican Beauty"

1954   "5 out of 25 City Pubs Bar Negroes and Mixed Couples"

1955   "Segregation Defended by CPR"

1956   "US Negro Freedom Drive 'Near Goal'"

1957   "Cleanup Underway on Skid Road"

1957   "First Negro Lawyer Called to Bar in BC Port"

1958   "This Was Freedom"

1959   "Negro Bus Driver Race-Group Head"

1960   "Freedom Built Negro Colony: Yankee Dollar Pulled It Down"

1962   "Anti-Negro Barnett Faces Picket Line"

1963   "I Am a Negro"

1963   "Integration Lesson on a BC Island"

1963   "Negro Job Hunt Fires US Crisis"

1964   "The Canadian Kind of Segregation"

1964   "Hogan's Alley No More"

1965   "Slum Project Means 1730 Must Move"

1965   "Displaced People Take News Calmly"

1965   "Alabammy in Blackface"

1965   "Negro Masons Unbiased"

1965   "Our Negroes: The Fewer The Safer"

1967   "Strathcona Survey Shows Classic Problems"

1967   "Barriers Falling, Says Negro"

1967   "A Racial Minority So Highly Visible"

1968   "'Revolution Necessary' Says Black Power Advocate"

1968   "Equality in BC Impresses Negroes"

1968   "Gun-toting Panthers Return to US"

1968   "Black Panthers Leave Victoria"

1968   "Whites Cause Race Riots, Black Panther Maintains"

1968   "Trotskyite Speaks for Black Power"

1968   "Six Angry, Disarmed Black Panthers Visit UBC"

1968   "'Panthers' Leave Gun at Border"

1968   "Black Americans Cheering 'Symbolic' African Revolution"

1968   "Doesn't Sedition Matter Any More?"

1968   "Nancy Backs Athletes 'Black Power' Salute"

1968   "Parkinson Says Send Blacks Home"

1968   "Parkinson Backs 'No Blacks' Plan"

1968   "Canadians Not as Prejudiced as Americans—Negro MP Says"

1968   "Negro Discrimination? No Complaints"

1968   "Parkinson's Law Gets Lambasting"

1968   "Negro Revolution 'Exposes Whites'"

1968   "Eldridge Cleaver: 'This Is War'"

1969   "Violence Not Goal"

1969   "Seattle Panther Boss Questioned at Airport"

1969   "Panther Leader Charges 'Harassment' at Border"

1969   "Immigration Man Denies Harassment"

1969   "Language Is Key in Negro Unrest"

1969   "First Negro Joins City Police Force"

1969   "Historic Negro Church Reopens Here"

1970   "City Gets First Negro Policeman"

1970   "Black Nigerian Finds Racial Prejudice"

1970   "Fired Over Color, Negro Hits Surrey Move"

1970   "Colored Issue Denied in Dismissal"

1970   "Black Problem a 'White Problem'"

1970   "African Student Complains of Housing Discrimination"

1970   "African Has a Home"

1970   "Canada's Blacks on March, Warns Civil Rights Leader"

1971   "Colored People Quizzed on Treatment in BC"

1971   "Many Blacks Fear Government"

1973   "Rosemary Brown Calls for Women's Ministry"

1973   "Landlady Faces Charges of Barring 'Black' Man"

1974 "Former Slave's Story Tells of Island's Early Days"

1978 "Back to the Basics of Being Black in Beautiful BC"

1978 "Job Picture 'Improved for Blacks'"

1978 "Story of Pioneer Blacks Fills Gap in History (Go Do Some Great Thing)"

1979 "Two Disco Staff Found Guilty of Assault"

1979 "New City Law Cracks Down on Discrimination in Clubs"

1979 "Blacks Plan Rally in Protest of 'Judicial Abortion'"

1979 "Cabaret Guilty of Turning Away Blacks: Misty's Fined in 1ˢᵗ Such BC Case"

1979 "Blacks Claim Discoes Are Charging Them Extra"

1979 "Disco Manager Sorry 'Innocent Blacks' Got Turned Away"

1979 "Racism in Vancouver"

1979 "Council Votes on Closing of Disco"

1980 "There's the Law … in Black and White"

1983 "Black Settlers To Get Tribute"

1985 "Province's Blacks Celebrate Their Past and Future"

1987 "Black Teenager's Shooting Death Revives Charges of Police Racism"

1990 "One of BC's Black Pioneers: A Big Man in Many Ways"

1992 "Black in BC"

1993 "Black Youth Being Unfairly Targeted, Report Claims"

1994 "Report Exposes RCMP Spying on Black Activists"

1995 "Vancouver Police Seek Ethnic Mix"

1995 "Census To Ask People To Identify Racial Origins"

2000 "Officer Who Brought Colour to the Force Retires After 30 Years"

2000 "Sociologist in Search of Naked Truth"

2003 "Visible Minorities Still Targeted"[32]

NOTES

1 *The Road Taken*, dir. Selwyn Jacob, DVD, National Film Board of Canada, 1996.
2 The area of Vancouver that I am referring to, which contained Hogan's Alley and is just east of Main Street from Prior Street to the Burrard Inlet, was traditionally known as "the East End." However, in his 1950 report, planner Leonard Marsh arbitrarily renamed the area "Strathcona" (*Rebuilding a Neighbourhood: Report on a Demonstration Slum-Clearance and Urban Rehabilitation Project in a Key Central Area in Vancouver* [Vancouver: University of British Columbia, 1950] 2). Today, the latter term remains official, although some still use the former. In this essay I will use "East End" when referring to the area before 1950, "Strathcona" when referring to it after 1950, and "East End/Strathcona" when referring to it across the decades.
3 The Hogan's Alley Memorial Project, "The Decommissioning of 823 Jackson Avenue, Once the African Methodist Episcopal Fountain Chapel," weblog entry, *Hogan's Alley Memorial Project: Memorializing Vancouver's Historic Black Neighbourhood and the Wider Vancouver Black Experience*, November 1, 2008, March 3, 2010 <http://hogansalleyproject.blogspot.com/2008/11/on-26-october-2008-basel-hakka-lutheran.html>.
4 Charleen P. Smith, "Boomtown Brothels in the Kootenays, 1895–1905," *People and Place: Historical Influences of Legal Culture*, eds. Jonathan Swainger and Constance Backhouse (Vancouver: University of British Columbia Press, 2004), 134. See also Lani Russworm, "The Elusive Hogan's Alley, Part 2," weblog entry, *Past Tense: Fragments of Vancouver History and Reflections Thereon*, August 5, 2008, August 1, 2009 <http://pasttensevancouver.wordpress.com /2008/04/05/the-elusive-hogans-alley-part-2/>, which covers the issue of Hogan's Alley's name in depth.
5 Jane Jacobs, *The Death and Life of Great American Cities* (New York: Vintage, 1992).
6 Mike Harcourt and Ken Cameron, *City Making in Paradise: Nine*

Decisions That Saved Vancouver (Vancouver: Douglas and McIntyre, 2007) 31–55.

7 "Hogan's Alley Before the Demolition," *City of Vancouver Archives-*July 16, 2009, August 1, 2009 <http://vancouver.ca/ctyclerk/archives/exhibits/HogansAlley/index.htm>; John Punter, *The Vancouver Achievement: Urban Planning and Design* (Vancouver: University of British Columbia Press, 2003), 25.

8 Interviews with Nora Hendrix, Rosa Pryor, Leona Risby, Austin Philips, and Dorothy Nealy in *Opening Doors: Vancouver's East End*, eds. Daphne Marlatt and Carole Itter (Victoria: Province of BC, Provincial Archives, 1979), 59–63, 108–10, 138–40, 140–44, 169–174; *Hogan's Alley*, dirs. Andrea Fatona and Cornelia Wyngaarden, videocassette, Video Out, 1994.

9 John Atkin, *Strathcona: Vancouver's First Neighbourhood* (North Vancouver: Whitecap, 1994), 77; "Militant Mothers of Raymur," *Viaduct*, June 25, 2008, August 1, 2009 <http://viaducteast.ca/2008/06/25/militant-mothers-of-raymur/>.

10 Crawford Kilian, *Go Do Some Great Thing: The Black Pioneers of British Columbia* (Burnaby, BC: Commodore, 2008).

11 "2006 Community Profiles: Vancouver: Visible Minority Population Characteristics," *Statistics Canada, February 5, 2010, March 22, 2010 <http://www12.statcan.ca/census-recensement/2006/dp-pd/prof/92-591/details/page.cfm?Lang=E&Geo1=CMA&Code1=933__&Geo2=PR&Code2=59&Data=Count&SearchText=Vancouver&SearchType=Begins&SearchPR=01&B1=Visible%20minority&Custom=>.*

12 See Rosemary Brown, *Being Brown: A Very Public Life* (Toronto: Random House, 1989), 12. In this passage of her memoir, Brown, the late New Democratic Party Member of Parliament, describes what seems to me to be typical of black British Columbians' mixed families: "My grandmother Imogene Wilson-James was the descendant of indentured workers from India who came to Jamaica after the abolition of slavery to work in the sugar cane fields. She married my grandfather Walter James, known to everyone as Pappy James, a

pharmacist, who was the product of the union of a white man and a Black woman. This multicultural beginning expanded until, by the time of my grandchildren's generation, it included Germans, Spanish Jews, Americans, Canadians, Chinese and a member of the Cree Nation."

13 Wayde Compton, ed., *Bluesprint: Black British Columbian Literature and Orature* (Vancouver: Arsenal Pulp, 2001).

14 See Janet Smith, "Reviving a Lost Black Heritage," *Georgia Straight* (February 20–27, 2003), 62.

15 See Chuck Davis, "Black Community of Strathcona and Hogan's Alley in Vancouver," *Vancouver Historical Society Newsletter* (March 2005), 4.

16 Jack Stepler, "Hogan's Alley Fate at Stake," *Vancouver Daily Province*, (April 21, 1939), 29.

17 Robin W. Winks, *The Blacks in Canada: A History*, 2nd ed. (Montreal-Kingston: McGill-Queen's UP, 1997), 416.

18 "Visible Minority Population Characteristics," British Columbia, *Statistics Canada*, July 24, 2009, August 1, 2009 <http://www12. statcan.ca/census-recensement/2006/dp-pd/prof/92-591/details/page. cfm?Lang=E&Geo1=CMA&Code1=933__&Geo2=PR&Code2=59 &Data=Count&SearchText=British%20Columbia&SearchType=B egins&SearchPR=01&B1=Visible%20minority&Custom=>; "Visible Minority Population Characteristics," Nova Scotia, *Statistics Canada*, July 24, 2009, August 1, 2009 <http://www12.statcan.ca/ census-recensement/2006/dp-pd/prof/92-591/details/page.cfm?Lang= E&Geo1=CMA&Code1=933__&Geo2=PR&Code2=12&Data=Cou nt&SearchText=Nova%20Scotia&SearchType=Begins&SearchPR=01 &B1=Visible%20minority&Custom=>.

19 Melinda Mollineaux, "Cadboro Bay Photographs," *Capilano Review* 2 no. 29 (Fall 1999), 47–56.

20 "Hogan's Alley Welcomes You," Lauren Marsden, personal home page, July 1, 2007, August 2009 <http://www.laurenmarsden.com/ imagepages/images_hogans.html>.

21 "Guerilla art and public memory," *Hogan's Alley Memorial Project:*

Memorializing Vancouver's Historic Black Neighbourhood and the Wider Vancouver Black Experience, weblog entry, July 9, 2007, August 1, 2009 <http://hogansalleyproject.blogspot.com/2007_07_01_archive.html>.

22 "Study shows Downtown Eastside housing situation is getting worse," *Carnegie Community Action Project*, weblog entry, June 17, 2009, August 1, 2009 <http://ccapvancouver.wordpress.com/2009/06/17/study-shows-downtown-eastside-housing-situation-is-getting-worse/>.

23 Monte Paulsen, "Vancouver Election Spending Out of Control," *The Tyee*, October 31, 2007, August 1, 2009 <http://thetyee.ca/News/2007/10/31/CityCampaignDollars/>.

24 *Fix: The Story of an Addicted City*, dir. Nettie Wild, DVD, Canada Wild Productions, 2002.

25 Ross Lambertson, "The Black, Brown, White and Red Blues: The Beating of Clarence Clemons," *Canadian Historical Review* 85 no. 4 (December 2004,: 769.

26 Crawford Kilian, *Go Do Some Great Thing: The Black Pioneers of British Columbia* (Burnaby, BC: Commodore, 2008), 143–44.

27 "Militant Mothers of Raymur," *Viaduct: Travels Through East Vancouver*, weblog entry, June 25, 2008, August 1, 2009 <http://viaducteast.ca/2008/06/25/militant-mothers-of-raymur/>.

28 "Woodsquat," special issue of *West Coast LINE* 41 (2003–04).

29 Advertisement, *Georgia Straight* 42 no. 2106 (May 1–8, 2008), 8.

30 "Province investigating condo developer Onni," *CTV British Columbia*, October 24, 25, 2008. <http://www.ctvbc.ctv.ca/servlet/an/local/CTVNews/20081024/BC_condos_real_estate_081024/20081024/?hub=BritishColumbiaHome>.

31 "Canada's Poorest Postal Code," weblog comment, "V6A: No condo for this postal code," *Condohype: Vancouver: Disown the Lifestyle*, weblog entry, October 24, 25, 2008. <http://condohype.wordpress.com/2008/10/24/v6a-no-condo-for-this-postal-code/>.

32 Newspaper headlines from the *Province* and the *Vancouver Sun*, 1900–2003, resulting from the search terms "Negroes," "Blacks,"

"Race Problems," "Hogan's Alley," "Slums," and "Visible Minority," using various research indices: BC Archives and Records Service Newspaper Index (BCARS), Northwest History Index, Public Libraries of British Columbia (BCPL), and Canadian Newsstand.

THE REPOSSESSION OF FRED BOOKER

In 1989, when I was seventeen years old, I stole the only thing I remember ever taking illegally during my entire youth: a single copy of a literary journal.

While as a teenager I had many friends who were as straight as rails, I had others who knew how to thieve like it was a fine art. I recall going into a record store with a classmate after school and coming out to find that he had not only stripped several cassette tapes of their security devices and stolen them, but that he had managed to put them into *my* pockets without me realizing it. Another friend preferred mugging. He was an oversized and tough kid, but he had an almost gentlemanly approach: he would walk up to someone who was sporting something flashy, like a new Walkman, and he would grab the kid by the arm, carefully explaining that he could either take a beating or just hand it over. If the kid gave up without a struggle, my friend would even pat him on the back as if to say, "Good choice. I knew you could do it," as he walked off with the prize. It was East Vancouver in the late 1980s, between the eras of heavy metal and gangster rap, so I was witness to a certain ratio of teenage criminality. But thievery wasn't really my thing. I wanted to write.

There was, in addition to joyful kleptomania, New Shoots, an experimental extracurricular high school program I'd joined. Through the Vancouver School Board, Creative Writing graduate students from the University of British Columbia facilitated once-a-week workshops at my school. My tutor was Leo McKay, Jr, a student then, but now a writer of acclaimed literary fiction who is based in Nova Scotia. Part of McKay's pedagogy was to get us teenagers reading current literary journals rather than canonical work, which, for me, was invaluable. When he gave me copies of various journals, I would read them cover-to-cover and over and over again.

I also recall, during those years, feeling an inchoate frustration about racism. Around that time I bought the hip hop album *It Takes a Nation of Millions To Hold Us Back* by Public Enemy, and it thoroughly rocked my sense of identity. Because Malcolm X and the Black Panthers are mentioned on that record, I made trips to the library to read about them.

By 1990, I walked through Vancouver with eyes newly opened to both literary journals and racial rebellion.

And so one afternoon when I scanned a bookshelf in one of my teachers' classrooms and saw an old copy of *PRISM international*, the University of British Columbia literary journal, I picked it up; when I read on the back cover that it featured "A selection of contemporary West African and Canadian Black (émigré) writing," I stole it. Two of my interests converged in that issue. Dialectical parts synthesized. On the one hand, I doubt the teacher would have minded that I took it, and he probably would have just given it to me, had I asked. On the other hand, I didn't think of asking. That issue, in that moment, made everything make sense, and I had to have it.

In its awkwardly worded blurb ("West African and Canadian Black (émigré) writing"?) I first perceived the notion of black literature here in Canada rather than in the United States, Africa, or the Caribbean. It was my first real sense of a localized black cultural production as opposed to the western Canadian sense that all blackness comes from elsewhere. At the time that I found it, the issue was already six years old— volume twenty-two, number four (July 1984)—and so was years ahead of the full bloom of Canadian identity politics. For that, the editors should be thanked: Richard Stevenson, Nona Kent, George McWhirter, *et al.* Some of the writers in that issue would become very important to me in later years: Dionne Brand, George Elliott Clarke, Lillian Allen, Claire Harris, M. Nourbese Philip, and Fred Booker.

I remember noting that Booker was the only writer in that issue whose biographical note placed him in British Columbia, and so he became the first black writer from *here* that I ever read. This is, in full, one of the poems printed in that issue:

> Some midwife who wore
> paint and jewelry made from teeth
> to boast
> left a pair of thumbprints
> on his scalp where no hair grows.

She checked his birth
ashamed of the legacy she left
white piracy of the dark continent
the rape of his mother, and
the lynching of faith, hope and charity.

He barely fought his way
from that abyss to this
under the lash of his father's black pride
and ambition for him to excel
like Martin Luther King Jr.

A shadow of the vernal dream
fleeing from a place which gave him
a reflection he couldn't accept
nearly dying in this foreign place
which gives him no reflection at all,

he takes his head in his hands
plants his fingers in those ancestral grooves
not knowing whether to pull or push. (1984, 68)

This text was just one of the many streams of information from which I drew in those years, so it wasn't until much later that I became conscious of its local significance. But I took the copy of the journal and carried it from home to home for years after each time I moved, out of my parents' house and into my first apartment, and so on. I went on to university, and the journal went with me. I had no intention of doing anything with it, but I knew that in those poems Booker phrased something I hadn't yet been able to articulate myself—it explained, in an incipient way, "this foreign place / which gives [us] no reflection at all." Booker was, for me, a hope of reflection.

The problem he put into print persists, though; all I knew to do then was to take, keep, possess, and repossess those words, in the way a reader does when a reader is in need.

Ten years later, after I had published my own book of poems, and while I was pursuing a Master of Arts degree in English at Simon Fraser University, I came upon the idea of editing a comprehensive anthology of black writers from British Columbia. This MA thesis project was eventually published as *Bluesprint: Black British Columbian Literature and Orature* (2001). During the preliminary research, I returned to that issue of *PRISM international*.

In a sense, my thesis hinged on Booker, along with two other writers, Truman Green and Christopher James. Because the history of black writing in BC is heavy with writing at the top and the bottom, like an hourglass, with a scant record of literature in the middle, it is the middle period over which I laboured most in my research. There were several black nineteenth-century writers who lived and wrote during and after the 1858 Fraser River Gold Rush, and, in the wake of a vibrant identity politics debate, numerous black writers started to appear in print in the 1990s. But in the period between, encompassing most of the twentieth century, there is relatively little black writing in this province.

In fact, if it weren't for Booker, Green, and James, who published during this "middle period," the literary history, as a book, would have bordered on incoherence. At the time, I was not certain that "black BC" was the most sensible formation for such a project; I considered a "black western Canadian" anthology, or perhaps a "black Pacific Northwest" collection. But the presence of Booker, Green, and James helped to link the pioneer era to the present. I continue to assert that "black BC" is really only a tool of a term—one that allows us to think and write about a context—rather than an essential identity formation. Those I call "black BC" authors belong also to other social and interpretive communities. Nevertheless, as an anthologist I needed writing in this "middle period" for morale in the course of my research, and to convince me that the project had an internal logic.

And, of these three—Booker, Green, and James—it is Booker whose work itself functions most clearly as a bridging force in the long collective project of black literature in this western-most province. A full two decades before C.S. Giscombe's *Giscome Road* (1998) and my *49ᵗʰ Parallel Psalm* (1999)—books of poetry that use the black history of the province as a subject—Booker wrote about the black pioneers in song lyrics such as "One Road to the Sea" from his record *Dear Jane: Book Three* (1978). This song is dedicated in part to the black matriarch of Salt Spring Island, Sylvia Estes Stark, and recounts her family's odyssey from the US to this part of Canada:

> A thousand and nine in gold
> To free my wife and child
> A lumber camp in Oregon
> Kept us for a while
> We heard about a place

North of Puget Sound
Where free men and the lion
Leave their prints upon the ground

Historical research, in fact, suffuses Booker's entire body of work. He wrote about black Canadian pioneers, with a particular focus on those in the west, in three forms: he published a substantial review in *Canadian Dimension* in 1979 on Grant MacEwan's biography *John Ware's Cow Country* (1960), about the famous Albertan rancher; he includes multiple allusions to Ware, Olivier Le Jeune, and Josiah Henson in his unpublished verse-novel, "Blue Notes of a White Girl"; and his short story "Matoxy Sixapeekwan" in *Adventures in Debt Collection* (2006) features a fictional protagonist descended from Ware who repossesses cars for a living a century later in Vancouver.

While I was researching Booker in 2000 for *Bluesprint*, the time came to seek permissions, and ordinary means of searching for him turned up nothing. So I had to do some detective work. Since one of Booker's records was dedicated to the novelist Jane Rule, I managed to track her down by phone, and though she had lost touch with Booker over the years, she connected me with another old friend in Winnipeg, who in turn finally gave me a current telephone number for Booker himself. When I finally talked to him, I explained the elaborate series of events that put me on his trail. He told me that he had spent years working, like his protagonist in "Matoxy Sixapeekwan," for a company that repossessed the vehicles of owners who had fallen behind in their payments. This job, Booker explained to me, required agents with tenacity and skill in tracking down quarry. He said I would have made a good "repo man" myself for having found him, since he had been "underground" since the 1970s. Later, after his work appeared in *Bluesprint* and he was introduced to many of the younger black writers in British Columbia today, Booker said to me that I had brought him back, that I had "repossessed" him.

This was a joke in his usual warmly humble style. But there was a touch of bitterness in it, too, a hint that he wished he'd made a bigger mark as a writer. At that time, in 2000, he had just turned sixty-one, and he'd never published a book, something he'd been diligently trying to do since the mid-1960s, when he first came to Canada from the US.

Booker told me that in the 1970s he wrote and performed music, touring across Canada, and that somewhere along the way he found himself in BC. Here he eventually produced and cut his own records, with help from Jane Rule, whom he'd befriended. But at the same time, he was working on his poetry for the page, which found its way into respected literary journals such as *The Fiddlehead*, *Quarry*, and, as mentioned, *PRISM international*. This attracted some attention. Lorris Elliott, the seminal critic of black Canadian writing, includes a biographical note on Booker in his groundbreaking *Literary Writing by Blacks in Canada: A Preliminary Survey* (1988).

When I asked him about those years, Booker told me he had promised himself at some point in the 1970s that he would publish a book before the end of that decade or he would quit writing and get a regular job. No more touring around the country and following the muse. But, he said, when a press initially accepted his manuscript and then went out of business, he was so discouraged that he decided to concentrate on his straight career and gave up the hot pursuit of literary publication. His straight job was, as it turned out, a career with General Motors, repossessing cars all across BC.

Such was the story that Booker initially told me, but, thinking about it now, I realize that the timeline does not work out. For example, Booker said that his manuscript for "Blue Notes of a White Girl" was accepted at Cacananadada Press, and that they asked him to wait a year for publication, and then after a year passed, they asked him to wait another year; then they went out of business, and resurfaced with new owners as Ronsdale Press in 1988. That places Booker's experience with Cacananadada between 1984 and 1988, meaning he was writing and revising through those years. And his first publication of a story from the manuscript that would eventually become *Adventures in Debt Collection* was in 1989, when an early version of "Matoxy Sixapeekwan" appeared in *Event*. Further publications of these stories appeared throughout the 1990s, in *Whetstone* (twice) and the *Windsor Review* in 1993, '95, and '98. In other words, Booker never stopped writing. When the Cacananadada lead fell through—it is unknown to me whether or not he ever signed a contract with them—Booker said that it devastated him. But, as far as the record bears out, it seems only to have caused him to switch forms, from poetry to fiction. Reflecting upon it now, I think the initial version of events

Fred Booker. Photo: Ian Smith/*Vancouver Sun*

Booker told me summed up his *feelings*—that he had wanted, for a moment at least, to give up. But the fact is that he did not.

After I published an excerpt from "Blue Notes of a White Girl" in *Bluesprint*, a cautious hope returned to Booker. I asked him if he was trying to get a book published. He was getting his stories into high quality literary journals—surely a book might follow? But he had been stung by his earlier experience, and admitted to me that he didn't send to publishers anymore, but that, yes, he wanted to have a book out before he died. This was by no means histrionics or rhetoric: before I'd met him, Booker had battled and defeated cancer of the larynx, and his doctors were concerned about a recurrence. Booker's trademark husky voice may have seemed to others like a former blues man's growl. But it was really a spoken scar.

I remember, when we mused about him publishing a book, probably in 2002 or '03, I nodded, wondering if it would happen, hoping it would. I had no idea at the time that he would indeed publish, and that I would become his publisher.

The concept of Commodore Books emerged out of several discussions I had with Glen Lowry at Coquitlam College, where we both taught English. Lowry, the editor of *West Coast LINE*, was considering extending the journal's mandate to include regular book publication. At the time I was also thinking about the *Bluesprint* project and how the next logical step seemed to be the creation of a black press. My hopes for *Bluesprint* were that it would put formerly neglected works in the public imagination, but that it would also stimulate new writing; a new black press would do the same. After a few years of dreaming and planning, the West Coast Review Publishing Society created LINEbooks; I asked Karina Vernon and David Chariandy—the two theorists of black Canadian writing I knew best—to join me as publishers, and Commodore Books was established as an imprint of LINEbooks. Thus we became the first black press in western Canada.

Throughout the conception of Commodore Books, I imagined Booker as our first author. He had shown me most of his unpublished work—his poetry, stories, and non-fiction. It was a difficult choice between asking him for the "Blue Notes of a White Girl" or "Adventures in Debt Collection" manuscripts, but ultimately I wanted to publish the latter because I felt that it was his most complex work. When he accepted, we immediately began the job of editing. I didn't ask for many substantial changes to his stories: we changed the titles of two of them; we dropped a final paragraph in one; we altered the order in which the stories appear. The most radical editorial decision was paring out several stories that seemed to me to be weaker than the rest. We didn't agree on everything, but it was a very amiable process.

Booker's wit appeared again at the launch of *Adventures in Debt Collection*, which we held at the Brickhouse Bar in Vancouver in November of 2006. There he said to the celebrants that it had taken him sixty-seven years to publish his first book and that he hoped it wouldn't take quite so long to publish his second.

Adventures in Debt Collection is clearly Booker's most important legacy as a writer. It is a volume of linked short stories, all connected by a fictitious financing company and the bailiff-protagonists who repossess cars on its behalf. But it is also about racism, sexism, class, and multiculturalism—and the *social* debts of Canada's colonial capitalism.

It isn't a book without faults. At times the prose strains to sing, and the quality of the stories is uneven. If you compare early stories (like "Matoxy Sixapeekwan") with ones written later (like "A Mask for Charlie Dan"), there is a tangible difference at the level of the sentence. There are occasional missteps, like the implausible premise of "Incident on Highway 3" in which the female protagonist vacations by hitchhiking alone across the province, apparently without any thought to her safety. Yet other stories, like "Woman of the Year," more convincingly address sexism as it appears in the workplace.

On the whole, though, *Adventures in Debt Collection* offers something unique. It is worth it, before moving into an analysis of its best moments, to explain two of Booker's objectives with the book, as I understand them.

When Booker retired from General Motors and set about writing these stories, he was anxious about them being seen as semi-autobiographical. Of course, as with all fiction, the author draws upon his experiences. But Booker was adamant that it was not a disguised tell-all about the job. He was committed to form and dedicated to fiction as his art.

Similarly, Booker wanted to avoid having his American origins over-determine his reception as a writer. He explained to

me his feeling that anti-black racism in Canada was mixed together with the treatment of black Canadians as perennial immigrants. In other words, although by the time we met, Booker
had lived in Canada longer than he had lived in the US, he
felt that white Canadians were more reluctant to consider him
Canadian than they would a white expatriate from the US.
Images of black America are so prevalent in Canada, Booker
explained, that he found his own experiences in this country
erased whenever anyone discovered he was born in Ohio. This
phenomenon is perhaps best expressed in the words of one
of Booker's characters, Creek Williams, a bailiff in the story
"Woman of the Year." Williams is a black Canadian by birth
whose boss, a judge,

> seemed incapable of interacting with Creek on any mat-
> ter other than their court business, or when a sensational
> news story broke involving blacks and violence in the
> US. If the big news story was Canadian and political, as
> when the country was involved in a national referendum
> or election, the judge refused to engage Creek in any
> meaningful conversation about it. Creek found this to
> be a common myopia among his white colleagues who
> sometimes treated him as they would a foreigner. When
> he was probed excitedly by someone hoping to expose
> him as an illegal American alien, Creek hoped to skewer
> the inquisitor with the information that his family had
> lived in British Columbia for over a century. Instead,
> Creek found that this fact was completely meaningless to
> the inquisitor, who preferred the inventions of his own

imagination. Long ago Creek had adapted to his isolation
as a perfect way to protect a rich privacy with his books
from which he was rarely disturbed. (Booker 2006, 51)

To avoid being over-associated with his American past,
Booker insisted that his author's biographical notes de-empha-
size his birthplace, saying, for example, that "Fred Booker has
been living and writing in Canada since 1966" (Booker 2006,
117). Booker's extensive research into and use of black Canadian pioneers in his writing reveal his deep identification with
this nation and its conditions. He understood the "indigenous"
black experience in Canada very thoroughly.

Indeed, seeds of Booker's thinking on national identity are
found in his 1979 review of *John Ware's Cow Country*. In this
text, Booker unthreads MacEwan's paternalistic biography of
Ware, who is, as Booker reads MacEwan's creation, "the Her-
cules, the Pied Piper and the golliwog of nineteenth century
Alberta" (50). He suggests that MacEwan's insistence upon
Ware's asexuality during years in which most Prairie men,
in the absence of endogamous prospects, took Native wives
or consorts, is mythical. And that MacEwan overemphasizes
Ware's physical feats and distorts his dialect, creating a figure
who is "a childlike, ignorant, powerless hulk [… reduced] to
the stature of a superior race horse" (51). When Booker states
early on in the review that "The book is gravely insulting to
the activist tradition of black Canadians and contradictory to
the abolitionist heritage of Canada in general as well as the
egalitarian record of western Canada in particular" (49), he

bespeaks a political position that holds up today: that in western Canada there is a particular black experience, that part of its voice can be found in its activism, and that anti-racist hope exists in linking it to broader movements. Furthermore, Booker cuts to the heart of the political use-value of racial myth to the white-supremacist Canadian state when he connects the tall tales of Ware to the reality of federal policy: "To make Ware's character child-like is to weaken him. I am convinced this device is deliberate. The intention is to include a flaw in the white public's memory of this black strong man. This flaw is necessary for those racist white Canadians who wish to maintain an egalitarian public image, but need at the same time a device to employ if it ever again becomes unpopular, as it did in Canada in 1911, to have blacks from the USA in large numbers immigrating to this country" (51). With a reference to Prime Minister Wilfrid Laurier's 1911 proposed legislation to ban black immigration—"For a period of one year from and after the date hereof the landing in Canada shall be [...] prohibited of any immigrants belonging to the Negro race, which race is deemed unsuitable to the climate and requirements of Canada" (in Shepherd 1997, 86)—Booker politicizes the battle over Ware's memory.

None of John Ware's six children reproduced, and so his line ended with his son Arthur Ware's death in 1989.[1] Booker's story "Matoxy Sixapeekwan"—titled after the Sarcee appellation for Ware, which means "bad black white man"—follows the story of Bob Ware, a fictional grandson of the great man. In this sense, it is an experimental story that asks us to imagine a western Canada from the point of view of Ware's descendent, a man who knows the myths attributed to his grandfather. Like Booker's review, the story applies pressure to the legend: if part of the white adulation of Ware depends upon him as a singular anomaly, what emerges if we instead imagine his progeny flourishing in the multicultural era?

For one, we find Booker's Bob Ware in Vancouver rather than southern Alberta, so the imagined progeny has drifted west. And instead of settling the plains and fighting the elements in a cowboy cliché, Bob's battles are against the glass ceiling in the realm of corporate financing:

> [... H]e didn't think that John Ware, monument as he was, would've succeeded any better than Bob had at crashing the white male party at the top of Worldwide Finance. But considering the legend, Bob thought that, likely, John would have battered himself against the gates of that exclusive place until he died rather than capitulate. All trainees at Worldwide were treated equally: whites, blacks, East Asians and East Indians, both genders. All were given hell on an equal basis. But the route to the upper ranks of the company was blocked to everyone except a white male elite. (2006, 11)

This is a theme that recurs throughout *Adventures in Debt Collection*. The employees of Worldwide Finance, and its contractors, are from a variety of backgrounds: two different black men, a Métis woman, a Japanese-Canadian man, a white woman, and two white men. All but the white men seem anxious about advancement or about their status as independent contractors.

Furthermore, John Ware's myth is a kind of Canadian answer to the genre of the American western, complicated by its central character's black identity. Similarly genre-inflected, Bob Ware stalks the owner of a delinquent Chevrolet Blazer through a cityscape and narrative plot that hints at the hard-boiled detective fiction of Dashiell Hammett or Raymond Chandler. Indeed, Booker's Vancouver is cloudy, shadowy, and *noir*, a place where we are told that "Main Street was a bold, direct line of commerce from the sawmills on the Fraser River, up the south slope, over the Mount Pleasant plateau, and down the north slope into the railway yards of Burrard Inlet. There the flashing red neon sign of the Red Lion Pub appeared like a stop sign warning against a reckless descent" (14). The detective work at the heart of this story and the others, centres, to varying degrees, upon the cat-and-mouse game of bailiff and defaultee, the latter often resorting to subterfuge to hide or keep the car. But what is most interesting in "Matoxy Sixapee-kwan" is that, in the end, Booker finally deflates the detective trope and, in the last paragraphs, introduces Bob Ware's own existential disinterest in the plot itself. After he has successfully solved the case and closed the account, he becomes uncertain about his mission, and, hence, his very identity:

> He thought that he'd have felt better about it if he'd truly
> accomplished something worthwhile. But he hadn't,
> because nothing had changed. He hadn't improved by

one precept [the defaultee's] moral character, or that of
anyone else. It was all meaningless, except for the fact
that this was what he did for a living, and that he did it
well.

If the legacy of John Ware was this simple, he thought—
skilled, dignified, independent action without the guar-
antee of the attainment of transcendence—then perhaps
there was a genuine link between himself and his revered
ancestor, whom his family canonized and whose enemies
named Matoxy Sixapeekwan. (17)

The anticlimax delivers a theme of futility and angst, suggesting a similar reading of the ambiguous role of the black
pioneers themselves. In the end, the real legacy of John Ware
(whom Booker refers to throughout as "the monument") seems
to be, for Bob at least, primarily ambivalent. Just as he is a
doubled "bad black white man"—both great and awful, black
and white, victim and agent of colonialism—like his grandfather, he is similarly an instrument of justice within a system
that he suspects is itself unjust. As John Ware's relationship to
the story of settlement and colonization is strained, so is Bob
Ware's situation in late capitalism. Exactly what "debt" is Bob
Ware collecting—the one that whites owe blacks for slavery?
The one that Canada owes to blacks for effectively closing the
door on immigration? Or does he simply believe it is his turn
to be the hammer rather than the nail in the construction of
the hegemony?

Throughout Booker's stories, this kind of investigation of

race and multiculturalism is the most interesting aspect. The *world* of Worldwide Finance is recognizably our own; it is certainly Vancouver and British Columbia, this topography, this ever-changing, lately colonized zone of unstable confluence. In "Woman of the Year," Booker captures, for example, the "availability heuristic" fallacy ("the tendency to judge the frequency or likelihood of an event by the ease with which relevant instances come to mind" [Baumeister and Bushman, 2010, 142]) that haunts perceptions of black presence in Vancouver, where the low percentage of the population who are black (about one percent) obscures the relatively high total number of blacks in the city (20,670).[2] When the character Rosemary Clarke, a white business woman, runs aground financially, she is warned that a black man, the bailiff Creek Williams, is seeking her in order to repossess her BMW, and suddenly, with this knowledge, Vancouver's demographic appearance transforms inexplicably before her eyes:

> [... S]he was gripped suddenly by a nauseating fear of her pursuer. He represented a factor previously unknown to her: an adversary who wasn't white. She had no black friends or associates, and, at that moment, could think of no black person's name. While driving the company van downtown to the Convention Centre, Rosemary's world filled up with black faces, and all of them seemed to be scrutinizing her: a black police officer sitting beside her in his car at a stop light; a black courier who rode the elevator with her up to the hotel lobby. She pulled the stack of brochures she carried close to her like a shield,

> stepping from the elevator into what appeared to be a
> nightmare. There were black people everywhere: at the
> front desk, in the lounge, at the magazine stand. Rose-
> mary tucked her head down, hoping to pass unnoticed.
> (57–58)

In a place with so little public discourse about how black people fit in our locality, Rosemary's sense of black absence in Vancouver veers wildly into overestimation, guided as it is by nothing more than her personal and immediate circumstances.

Similarly, in the story "Nativity," Booker rearranges the tableau of Christ's birth into a study of Canadian multiculturalism. The story's five major characters are each of a different race and region: a Japanese Canadian from Alberta; a black Maritimer; a white Edmontonian; a South Asian Vancouverite; and a member of the Shuswap First Nation from Kamloops. The multiracial co-owners of Conestoga Collections (an affiliate of Worldwide Finance) are the Three Wise Men to the Indian (of both sorts) Joseph and Mary, parents of Emma, a mixed-race Messiah figure and allusion. The story unfolds in BC's Cariboo region, where a love triangle subplot gives way to a story of reconciliation in the form of an "intentional family" relationship. The mother of the child, Mary (formerly Mahakali), asks Caspar, who has no family of his own, to be her daughter's unofficial adoptive grandfather. Although this is what Caspar wants more than anything, he expresses doubts that the child will bond with him:

"I'm afraid, Mary. I'm not her real granddad. I'm afraid
I'll lose her after all it's taken to have her."

"Who's real, Caspar: the family of your birth or the
family you chose? Do you consider your blood relatives
more important to you than Mel and Billy? Would you
give them up for anyone you left back home? Blood is
not thicker than the commitments we make. You chose
your brothers. I choose my father. Why is the choice less
genuine just because there's a different family member
chosen? If you will love her, then you are the greatest
granddad of all because you choose to be."

"But I keep asking myself, 'Why me?'"

"Why not you, Caspar? Because you were chosen, that's
why. Sometimes life's like that. You're chosen, and sometimes you're chosen for something you want." (78)

And it is here that Booker makes his point—through a redef-
inition of western civilization's primary scene—that multiculturalism-from-below is a process of deliberate and intentional
familiarity with little regard for blood, clan, or national origin.
The story ends on a decidedly hopeful image of mixed-race
and cross-cultural social improvisation in the heart of the rural
west.

But I believe the final story of *Adventures in Debt Collection*, "A Mask for Charlie Dan," is the best single piece of writing in the book. Interestingly, it doesn't feature black characters, but does configure perhaps the most intricate analysis of
race and culture in Booker's oeuvre. In this story, the Japanese-

Canadian character Melchior Komatsu from "Nativity" reappears, this time working alone and charged with the job of collecting payment for a Nissan truck that has been wrecked by an uninsured and delinquent owner named Charlie Dan. Mel drives into the remote northern British Columbian Takla reserve looking for this man and, like Bob Ware and Creek Williams in the earlier stories, finds himself to be an oblique factor in the local equation of tense racial animosities. As he enters the reserve, the pseudo-border crossing scene is disrupted by the ambiguity of his racial position:

> Over the gates to the Takla reserve was a sign reading
>
> ### WHITES KEEP OUT
>
> in lettering so enormous, and so imperatively red, it
> appeared as if it had been written with the blood of a
> thoughtless white trespasser. Mel's experience as a bailiff
> assured him that the sign was ritualized aggression, so
> without excessive caution he drove his GMC 4x4 through
> the open gates. Besides, he thought, the warning exclud-
> ed him. He wasn't a white man. (106)

Again, the question of this racialized bailiff's relationship to Canadian capitalism appears open, but the overlapping ironies multiply. Early on we are told that Mel's father and grandfather were Anglican clergymen who expected him to follow them in their vocation, and that he disappointed them by breaking with the tradition. It is also evident that Mel lived through the era of the Japanese-Canadian internment and forced resettlement, probably from BC to Alberta. As Mel's detective work on the reserve proceeds, he believes he is on the trail of Charlie Dan, only to discover dead-end after dead-end. An elder, who is following him, in a seeming non sequitur, tells Mel that he was physically assaulted by his own son, showing him a scar on his chest. As Booker notes, "Mel knew that conventions had changed for First Nations, as they had for many others; that the deference one was taught in the past to show to one's elders, especially toward one's father and uncles, no longer controlled the young. But to assault one's father to the extent that this boy had done wasn't merely a break with the past. It was an attempt to annihilate it" (107).

Wherever he goes, Mel finds that when he asks for Charlie Dan he is met with confusing answers like "Are you serious?" (107) or "He buys the beer when he's got money" (110) or he is simply laughed at; nevertheless, he is directed to the job-training centre, the hotel bar, or the sawmill, where he is told he may find the man. As Mel chases this ghost of a character, the elder follows him, ignored until finally the elder reveals to Mel that "Charlie Dan" is a name that men of the Takla Nation use to camouflage themselves within the white bureaucracy, a name like "John Doe" or "Joe Bloggs" among themselves, but a name that the white world takes seriously when it is used for legal purposes, shielding the signatory from consequence; it is a name and a mask. The elder's revelation, couched in myth, refers to the original Charlie Dan as a hero who disappears, Jonah-like, into the belly of a giant steelhead trout. (The scene also echoes a passage in Longfellow's *Song of Hiawatha* [1855] wherein the protagonist is swallowed by a giant sturgeon.)

At this moment, Mel's identity both threatens to pull apart and promises a new formation: he realizes that the mistake he made was to ignore the elder—an error he should have known better than to have made, for we discover that Mel, as a youth, went through a phase in which his circle of friends were Native, back in Alberta, and that he actually tried for a time to "pass" as Native himself, "growing his hair long, then braiding it with rawhide in the warrior-style of his two Cree friends, making it difficult for many to tell the three of them apart" (113). These friends, we are told, taught Mel the Native tradition of respecting and listening to elders—not terribly different from Japanese values—and he realizes in this scene the value of that lesson. Suddenly the journey of repossession causes him to reflect upon his own divergence from his father's life. Near the very end of the story, Mel pauses to drink from a river at the side of the road and sees his reflection in the water. In this moment he realizes that, while he believed he was chasing a defaultee, he is really seeking an aspect of himself—an implied reconciliation with his father. And, in the process of giving up the repossession, he defers to the far richer world of the imagination: "As ridiculous as it might seem, Mel thought that it would serve Worldwide just as well if he wrote in his report that, like Jonah, Charlie Dan had been swallowed by a large fish. Because he was certain that even under oath, in a court of law, no government or corporate authority would succeed in extracting from any member of the Takla Nation a more credible story than this one" (114). Mel finally departs the reserve with an identity that is pricelessly disrupted. The case stays open, and the book ends on this note. The agent abandons retribution, and finds agency.

Those last words that I quote above, about the character Mel Komatsu, are the final words Booker published in his lifetime.

After the launch of *Adventures in Debt Collection*, he did as much as he could to promote the book, doing readings and classroom appearances where it was being taught, and participating in conferences. Periodically he would inform me of his recurrences of cancer. And though I understood how serious it was, Booker always had a way of making it seem surmountable and, sure enough, I would see him again after rounds of radiation and chemotherapy, at a reading, book launch, or for our regular lunches in a restaurant near Coquitlam College, where we would meet during my breaks between classes. I got so used to the way Booker would shake off these recurrences that it came as a sudden shock when his wife, Monique, informed me that after his latest round of chemotherapy, in a weakened state, he contracted pneumonia and died in Burnaby General Hospital on June 4, 2008. He was sixty-nine years old.

My own claim on Booker is as a younger writer of African descent who felt a need for models, precedents, and foundations. In his work, I saw a platform, an origin from which to work, and this has made my project of cultural imagination easier. The fact that his vision was nuanced and engaged is a bonus for which I am grateful.

While the federal powers can claim an official Canadian multiculturalism—which they variously starve or manipulate according to the shifting winds of policy—there has always been a multiculturalism-from-below that works for diversity with or without state sanction. Booker was part of that movement, as seen in his literary efforts discussed here. But he very nearly missed the multicultural dividend, the phenomenon which put into print those who worked in isolation or whose work came before identity politics won the argument for self-representation outside the colonial myth of "two founding nations." Booker's achievement is, I think, the writing of a black identity in the integrated West as a complex, various, and overlapping subject position, one that is always in play with *other* others, so to speak. In reading him we discover, like his character Mel, that embracing the open case, rather than pursuing resolution, can be the most direct route to wisdom.

NOTES

1 "The Legend of John Ware," *Alberta Centennial*, Government of Alberta, 2002, June 25, 2008 <http://www.albertacentennial.ca/history/viewpost.aspx~id=245.html>.
2 "2006 Community Profiles: Vancouver: Visible Minority Population Characteristics," *Statistics Canada*, February 5, 2010, March 22, 2010 <http://www12.statcan.ca/census-recensement/2006/dp-pd/prof/92-591/details/page.cfm?Lang=E&Geo1=CMA&Code1=933__&Geo2=PR&Code2=59&Data=Count&SearchText=Vancouver&SearchType=Begins&SearchPR=01&B1=Visible%20minority&Custom=>.

ALEXIS MAZURIN, THE HOT SAUCE POSSE, AND BLACK HISTORY MONTH ON THE EDGE

HISTORY AND BUNK

Looking at old black-and-white photographs of Carter G. Woodson, the man who invented Negro History Week in 1926, it's hard to locate a flicker of humour in his features. That's understandable. In terms of the long march toward equality, ancestors such as Woodson did the heavy (up)lifting. And due to their work, we of later generations can take for granted legacies—including Black History Month—that continue to chip away at white supremacy.

Black North Americans have had many reasons to be wary of the mixture of comedy and politics. The informal name given to segregation in the United States—Jim Crow—was, after all, derived from the name of a clownish black caricature common in white-authored minstrel shows. So in Woodson's time, the call for black inclusion was serious business. But today, in light of the mixed success of integration (no pun intended), black representational terrain seems less like a battleground and more like the shifting floor at a funhouse.

In 2005 Alexis Mazurin, the Canadian Broadcasting Corporation (CBC) radio journalist and comedian, died at the young age of twenty-seven. While it's not accurate to say I was a close friend of Mazurin's, I admired his work. I enjoyed his radio presence, and followed the rowdy and controversial live-comedy group he belonged to, the Hot Sauce Posse. When I heard on September 5, 2005 that Mazurin had had a heart attack in the Nevada desert at the annual Burning Man Festival, I was stunned. The heart attack put him into a coma from which he never recovered, and he died October 20 at St Paul's Hospital in Vancouver.

I can count the number of times I met Mazurin in person on one hand, and three of my memories of him come from successive Black History Month events. I first met Mazurin at the now-closed Big Al's Cajun and Soul Food Restaurant on First Avenue in Vancouver, during a Black History Month opening ceremony. Another year, he called me up seeking contact information for a radio show he was putting together in February, on which he wanted to feature some former residents of the old black community of Hogan's Alley. And I saw Mazurin and the Hot Sauce Posse perform at Vancouver's Railway Club during the Month—an event nominally celebrating Black History which, in typical Mazurin-and-crew fashion, stirred the ideological pot more than it invoked anybody's sense of unity.

Recalling him this way—through Black History Month events—feels ironic because Mazurin seemed uncomfortable with the very concept. He was wary of pro-black stridency in general. The one in-depth conversation I ever had with him was about how little patience he had for the "blacker than thou" pressures he felt from certain Afrocentric circles. This skepticism was reflected in his comedy. He joked about being as Russian as he was black—and would then order a cocktail, the Black Russian. He joked about his own unrepentant record of dating "outside the race"—and wondered if a mulatto, by definition, ever can date "within" his race. Mazurin, like any thinking person, was troubled by notions of purity and was quick to look for contradictions in their structures.

It wasn't that Mazurin didn't identify as black—he did. He practiced capoeira, the African-Brazilian martial art, a form afforded high cultural status amongst Afrocentrists. But Mazurin seemed ambivalent about black activism, as such. This is what I learned about him from the first conversation we had. Despite his stated reticence that night, most of the other times I spoke to him were in some way linked to Black History Month. He may have had misgivings, but Mazurin did participate. Whatever he thought of intentional ethnicity, he believed the call was worth an involved response. And if the call itself wasn't to his liking, he switched up the tune. The edgy comedy he and the Hot Sauce Posse created was the synthesis of all this racial pressure and subjective subversion.

GOOKS AND SPOOKS

The Hot Sauce Posse was a mix of CBC-orbiting personalities and other local performers, including Mazurin, Tetsuro Shigematsu, J.J. Lee, Charlie Cho, Sharon Nam, Sumi Nam, Amy Wong, Philip Gurney, and Bahareh Shigematsu. It was

Vancouver-based, ethnically mixed, and demographically top-heavy with Asians. Who had ever heard of a Canadian comedy group like this? They were not multicultural in a state-sanctioned sense, but more like a video of Visible Minorities Gone Wild.

The Hot Sauce Posse was decidedly "blue," in the way people used to call Redd Foxx records blue, with four-letter words and racial epithets a-flyin'. The first I heard of the group was in 2002, when Charlie Cho slipped me a flyer for their show at Nic's Garage during the Vancouver Fringe Festival. The flyer featured two racial caricatures, a bucktoothed cartoon "Oriental," complete with conical hat and bayonet-fitted rifle, and the immortal image of Little Black Sambo, ever poised to bite into his slice of August ham, like Tantalus. Their show was called "Gooks and Spooks." How could I *not* go?

Sitting in that garage-cum-theatre, I was shocked and stunned. The Hot Sauce Posse in action was like an Afro-Asiatic Kids in the Hall, but rawer—more "slack," as the Caribbeans say. Each sketch was shot through with racial and sexual irreverence. Before my eyes, the Siamese Twins Chang and Eng argued over the logistics of one of them patronizing a prostitute. A "Chigger" (you figure it out) fronted in hip hop dialect to his black friend about pimping his own grandmother, until she finally clued into what he was saying and cussed him out in Chinglish. Two *Maxim*-buying yobs, black and white, coolly concluded that their lives would be better if they were gay— Mazurin and Gurney simulated it "doggy style," all the while dispassionately debating the pros and cons of their defection.

The Hot Sauce Posse, from left to right: Charlie Cho, J.J. Lee, Sharon Nam,
Alexis Mazurin, Tetsuro Shigematsu, Bahareh Shigematsu, Philip Gurney, Amy
Wong, and Sumi Nam. Photo: Troy Gray

The audience laughed and squirmed all through the show. I
saw a woman with her hands over her eyes, watching through
her fingers like one does a horror movie. The audience seemed
tense and uncertain if it was okay to laugh, so when the gags
were too funny to deny, the laughter came out in bursts—you
could hear the pent-up release, the nervousness that the laughter was shattering.

I am reminded of the debates about the origins of laughter itself. Some scholars have suggested that laughter is related
to fear and danger, that it's a sort of signal that something
seemingly frightening is just in jest, a kind breathy release of

tension.[1] Maybe laughter is a cousin of the "fight or flight" instinct. A joke is, essentially, a transgressive presentation of a contrived mistake, a transparent social miscue. We laugh when our expectations are thwarted in a turn of phrase that skips across the surface of understood social propriety. In the middle of a social paradox, a little bit scared and a little bit boggled, we laugh instead of attacking or running away.

So perhaps comedy, at its heart, is supposed to scare the crap out of you. And what is scarier than race? Contrary to the fact that laughter is supposed to be a *substitute* for flight, the last time I saw Mazurin and the Hot Sauce Posse perform at the Railway Club for Black History Month, people did flee. Some of the audience walked out.

This took place when the Posse did a karaoke version of comedy, in which they took turns "covering" famous routines. In one scene, the token white Posse member, Gurney, performed Chris Rock's auto-epithetical "Niggas vs. Black People" monologue word-for-word.[2] (This was a Black History Month event, I remind you.) While black people are given a pass for using the word "nigger," to whites it is *verboten*, even, it seems, when the white person is actually quoting a black person, and has said so—which was the genius of the piece, the hilarious contradiction, and the social comment.

Nevertheless, back-channel arguments about the event rippled through my e-mail browser for weeks afterward. I tried my best to argue that the butt of the sketch's humour was clearly, if you peel back the layers, the goofiness of wiggerism. It was about how an epithet changes according to the space, place, speaker, and context. It was about how Afrophilia and Afrophobia become harder to distinguish as the years go by, as African-American culture goes global, and white youths internalize black abjection. (The sketch could have been titled "Archie Bunker's Grandson Plays Chris Rock.")

What was also lost on the offended audience members, I think, was that Mazurin was there on the stage, too, overseeing Gurney's character as he put his Caucasoid foot in his Ebonic mouth. Knowing Mazurin, he was the one who, when they were jamming on the idea earlier, laughed the loudest, and said, "Oh yeah, let's do it." This is how he celebrated black history: by messing with your head. Mazurin observed the Month by satirizing its orthodoxies.

THE ANTI-MODEL-MINORITY
The Hot Sauce Posse had been in an uncertain state before Mazurin's heart attack, and since his death, it seems unlikely to continue as a group. But while they were going strong, I had hopes that they might have become the same sort of harbinger for Canada that Richard Pryor's explosive record *That Nigger's Crazy* (1974) was for the US—in other words, a signal that the nation's resident minorities are officially and irrevocably uppity en masse. Pryor's death, just a couple of months after Mazurin's, made a strange cross-border rhyme.

I looked to Mazurin and the Hot Sauce Posse's work for signals about our nation, just as early fans of Pryor might have sensed his prophetic qualities regarding their republic. Black Power and its signs pop up throughout Pryor's oeuvre, from a marginal reference to the Black Panthers in *Live and Smokin'* (1971) to his respectful hailing of Huey P. Newton himself, an audience member at the filming of *Live in Concert* (1979). As an adjunct to the stiflingly serious Movement, Pryor represented the popular culture's response to the fall of official racism: blacks announced themselves as out of control in every sense. The resultant revelry after that lifting of expressive repression can still be heard in the vocal explosion of hip hop today.

In Canada, the land of cooler heads prevailing, official 1970s Liberal Party-defined multiculturalism might have given us a similar go-ahead for comedic minority shit-disturbing. But it took until the 1990s and Thomas King's CBC radio show *Dead Dog Café Comedy Hour* to get us some of that taboo-smashing, racial self-examination that only humour can deliver. (Russell Peters may be the current heir to this position.) I think that having the Hot Sauce Posse to deal with, as a nation, might have been seismic. Call it hyperbole, but I see a direct line between 1990s queer media infiltration (via Scott Thompson and *The Kids in the Hall*) and the legalization of same-sex marriage a decade later. If you can buy that, what do you think might also have been in store for us if a bunch of anti-model-minorities like these had been unleashed upon our unsuspecting racial and sexual national consciousness?

What I particularly admired about Mazurin and the Hot Sauce Posse's style was the way that, like Pryor and Lenny Bruce before them, they practised a comedy that verged on Antonin Artaud's concept of Theatre of Cruelty—a performance that assaulted the audience, that provoked them as a way of making plain their personal stake in the events taking place on the stage; as a way of reminding them that a seat in the crowd is not a bubble which protects you from the world. Bruce sometimes harangued his audience to the point of frenzy. Pryor made you unsure at times if you were supposed to laugh, weep, or walk out.

I believe Mazurin was after this effect, too, and he wanted his audience—black, white, Asian, all—to feel disconfirmed in their notions of ethnicity and self. He wanted them to feel as up in the air as he did, as exposed as a racialized individual in this world sometimes feels: open and implicated. His contribution to black history might not be of the capital-letter variety, the kind that flies the red, black, and green. But I will miss the levelling humour that Mazurin offered, the laughs that any serious-as-cancer activism needs to keep it from drifting into Robespierre territory. That's one crucial service that prurient, scatological, mischievous line-crossers can provide. A movement needs both activists and satirists—the latter keep the former humble.

That first conversation I had with Mazurin, in which he expressed his uncertainty about Black History Month, was interrupted, and so I never got to hear what exactly the nature of his concern was. The host of the event got the show on the road and, as chance would have it, over the next few years, Mazurin and I never wound up in a similarly deep conversation. But as a fan, I heard his comedy as the latter half of that discussion. And though I'll miss him making me laugh, I won't forget how spectacularly he made his point.

NOTES

1 "Behavioural biology expert puts forward theory of why we laugh," *guardian.co.uk*, June 4, 2009, March 5, 2010 <http://www.guardian. co.uk/science/2009/jun/04/why-laughter-behavioural-biology>.

2 It was also at least a year before the US television situation comedy *The Office* did a similar bit ("Diversity Day," *The Office*, NBC, March 29, 2005).

TURNTABLE POETRY, MIXED-RACE, AND SCHIZOPHONOPHILIA

PHONO/SOUND/GRAPH/WRITING

Jason de Couto hits the sampler button, starting a recorded excerpt from skeptic and science-journalist Brian Dunning's podcast.

Dunning's voice emerges from the speakers. In this sample, he discusses sine waves—randomly modulated synthetic sounds—and how some people think they hear paranormal messages in them, so-called "electronic voice phenomena." Dunning introduces a series of sine waves, which sound like mere noise, and then immediately afterward he plays a woman's voice talking and modulating her words similarly to the waves. Then he plays the sine waves again. While at first the sine waves sounded meaningless, now—having heard the woman speak just after hearing the waves—one seems to perceive her words within what were previously nonsensical squawks. It is like a sonic version of a visual afterimage. This phenomenon, Dunning tells us in the sample, is known as "pareidolia," the innate human susceptibility to finding patterns in naturally random stimulus, like seeing faces or the bordered shapes of nations in passing clouds.

In my view, human features—hair, skin, eyes—are also naturally random. Race is pareidolia: a trick of the eyes, an imposition of the imagination.

At the same time as he cues the Dunning sample, de Couto also starts the instrumental song "Awaiting an Accident" by Boom Bip on his right turntable. The track begins quietly, with a repeating bell and an electronic howl that both gradually build in volume and complexity toward the introduction of a full beat, which arrives with a thunderous kick drum. Throughout the buildup, de Couto scratches quietly in the background on his left turntable on an electronic beep from Qbert's *Secret of the Y Formula*. It mimics the sound of Dunning's sine waves. De Couto's scratching is an ironic commentary on Dunning's analysis of drawing meaning out of non-meaning; his scratching is like an active, intuitive form of pareidolia. Whereas a pareidoliac finds a face in the rocks randomly strewn about the surface of Mars, de Couto, on the other hand, is building an inukshuk.

When the full Boom Bip beat kicks in, it is my cue to start the sample of my poem "The Reinventing Wheel" on the one. I cue it up and spin the dub plate containing my vocal recording at the stanza that begins,

> Lyrical / prosaic,
> settler / native,

> American / North American,
> nationalism / segregation (2004, 105)

and I play these, my own words and voice, which are recorded on this acetate, on my right turntable. To the question of pareidolia, I match these lines, which I first intended to suggest a list of false binaries that defy hard separation. The sample ends with a list of terms for mixed-race people:

> mulatto,
> mestizo,
> métis,
> cabra,
> Eurasian,
> creole,
> coloured (105)

When I kill the volume on my mixer, stopping my poem at a natural pause, de Couto cuts the power on his right turntable so that the track decelerates into a blur of sound. Then he scratches in the "Dial 7" instrumental track by Digable Planets on his left turntable, mixing it into the auditory smear of the former slowing sample.

At the beginning of the second bar, I start a track on my left turntable, from the record *Alex Haley Tells the Story of His Search for Roots* (1977). It is a moment in which Haley, lecturing about his famous book, describes an experience in Africa of realizing, seemingly for the first time, that he has white ancestry, comparing his brown skin-colour to his African kinsmen's significantly darker complexions. Haley's voice is stentorian and Southern as he describes an experience that sounds like a full-blown anxiety attack. He finally says, "I was standing there being rocked by that—" and I downfade the volume there, mid-sentence. De Couto picks it up on his sampler, where he has loaded those same words—"rocked by that"—which he rhythmically trills over the beat for a bar or so, repeating it again and again, by pressing a button: "rocked by, rocked by, rocked by that."

Then he cues and starts the song "Ha-doh" by DJ Krush and Toshinori Kondo on his left turntable, fading out "Dial 7." I return to my right turntable where I match to it the section of my poem that begins, "Act like you know. / I take my cue out of crates and boxes, / speak by outfoxing rock" (108), letting the dub plate spin through four stanzas of verse.

De Couto mixes in the next instrumental track, "Eggroll Suite," by Live Human, a low wash of bass punctuated by intermittent toms and a sinister synthetic trumpet sound. It is sparse and ominous and builds in volume as it proceeds. I cue a track titled "Vancouver and Racial Violence (1886–1907)" from a record cut in 1971 to commemorate the centennial of British Columbia's entrance into Canada as a province. The narrator describes the anti-Asian riots in detail and debunks the myth of "the Yellow Peril," recasting it as a racist response to "an industrious people quietly minding their own business."

Finally, de Couto blends in the beautifully languid "Atma" by Michał Urbaniak on his right deck, while I drop the last selection of my poem, which begins, "Up from my vestigial vinyl lobe, Blow" (107)—an inquiry into the apathy and accident of hip hop music made far from its place of origin. The three selections of my poem that I have used for this performance are out of order from their recording and writing, and are only a fraction of the whole poem. This last one, I hope, calls the audience back to the idea and presence of the turntables themselves.

At the end of the poetry sample, I downfade the volume, and de Couto starts his longest scratch solo of the set. He alternates between the electronic beep, which recalls the initial sine waves, and a sample of a human gasp. He cuts and chops these two sounds, back and forth, making music out of these juxtaposed bits of noise. The Urbaniak track moves to a crescendo. (Most tracks do, I realize, and so a performance stitched together out of them resembles a tide and its waves, crashing in, and then quietly receding.) Just before the last notes of "Atma" fade, I cue an epigraph from a section of my poem, my voice speaking the 3,000-year-old words from Lamentations 1:1 and 5:21. To me, these words are, anachronistically, about urban renewal, fractured tradition, and revolution: "How doth the city sit solitary, that was full of people! [...] Turn thou us unto thee, O Lord, and we shall be turned; renew our days as of old." The awkward syntax of the latter verse is like a halting cueing/back-cueing scratch, and we arrive at the beginning, the source, the lament before the lament, the loss before the loss, the sonic homecoming.[1]

The author and Jason de Couto performing during the
"interior Investigations" convergence, Kamloops, BC,
2006. Photo: Ashok Mathur

Jason de Couto and the author performing at the Vancouver
Art Gallery in 2006. Photo: Sita Kumar

BEAUTIFUL INAUTHENTICITIES

The previous piece is a précis of our performance of "The Reinventing Wheel: A Turntable Poem" at the 2008 Scream in High Park Literary Festival in Toronto. I began the earliest form of this poem in 2000, and it has continually evolved over the years. In various venues, including classrooms, art galleries, and nightclubs, and with either choreographed or improvised sets, I have conducted live audio mixes of pre-recorded hip hop, jazz, spoken word, and dub plate recordings of my own poetry written specifically for this project. In the poem's earliest incarnations, I performed alone with two turntables. But lately the project has expanded to include Jason de Couto as my equal collaborative partner—we work together under the name the Contact Zone Crew, referring to Marie Louise Pratt's seminal essay on culture under colonialism[2]—and we use up to six turntables, sometimes including a Numark CDX digital turntable, and sometimes a sampler. In our pre-planned sets, every track and sample is meticulously decided upon beforehand, with the cues mapped out nearly to the second; but in our improvisational performances we choose a limited number of tracks beforehand and arrange the mix spontaneously. (The précis here is an example of the former kind of set.) Because the performance involves extensive use of copyrighted material by other artists, when it came time to publish my book *Performance Bond* (2004), which includes a CD, I chose to use a version that employs only samples from the public domain. For that I collaborated with Trevor Thompson, who composed the music, and we arranged and produced the track together at his home studio in Vancouver.

I wrote the text of the poem as an exploration of the meaning of hip hop, electronic culture, mixed-race, Ebonics as a second language, and black identity in western Canada. I was interested in examining how hip hop evinces a shift in the black literary tradition of connecting form to the people's music—how, whereas Langston Hughes and the New Negro Movement specifically drew influence from the blues, and Amiri Baraka and the Black Arts Movement used jazz as a formal influence, attempting to use hip hop in a similar way presents unique problems and opportunities.

While the New Negro Movement and the Black Arts Movement and their musical concomitants produced unique vocabularies and idioms, these vocabularies were relatively slow to evolve and were disseminated gradually across North America. In contrast, hip hop's facilitation and creation of new vernaculars has been accelerated because of several factors: the globalization of American culture (or cultural imperialism); the dissemination of electronic and digital reproduction technologies; and what might be called postmodern "re-mix culture"—the pervasive use of sampling in contemporary music. The in-group quality of black speech has become, by the very acceleration of the subculture's musical dissemination, de-territorialized. Black American slang is used and re-wrought everywhere, from New York to Accra to Berlin to Tokyo to Rio de Janeiro.

And to *my* Vancouver: there is a corollary here between the global denaturing of hip hop and the black experience itself in western Canada—a periphery of the diaspora—and perhaps between all isolated pockets of black culture that exist, whether in Vancouver, Stockholm, Glasgow, or Taipei—whatever cities or areas one does not think of as historically black centres. In these places of relatively sparse black population, the musical version of the vernacular transmits through hip hop in much the same manner as it does anywhere else—within the capitalist media and its electronic reproduction as much as through proximate socialization. A new development in hip hop culture from Los Angeles is as likely to arrive in New York, Kingston, London, or Johannesburg through electronic relay as by direct voice-to-ear interaction. Even in this age of migration, the sound moves eminently faster, farther, and more frequently than do people. So an opportunity exists in turntablism—the trope of hip hop fragmentation—to employ the inevitable and beautiful "inauthenticities" that these conditions of inorganic reception encourage. If, as Frantz Fanon suggests, the self-seeking return to "native" forms is regressive,[3] then perhaps in this electronic cultural shuffle there is an opportunity for the creation of newer, progressive concepts in the sound.

BROKEN AND RE-BROKEN

As a formal experiment, I had three initial goals for "The Re-inventing Wheel":

1. To make the voiced poem an art-object, outside of my body.
2. To change the trajectory of standard spoken word performance: rather than performing *from* the body, to let the body perform *upon* the work. (When I handle one of the dub

plates, my fingers touch a physical impression of my voice.)
3. To view my own poem as an external or found sample, and even as an object of *détournement*.

I'll briefly examine each of these three points of experimentation or experiential research.

My goal of dislocating the poem from my body in performance was an easy enough task, as a dub plate recording becomes an art object immediately upon being pressed. It is even a kind of auto-destructive art: a dub plate is an aluminum disc covered with acetate, a compound that degrades far more easily than vinyl. Dub plates were, in the days before the audiocassette, the easiest way to make a test pressing, or preview, of a professional record; dub plates linger on as the cheapest, quickest method of making a very small amount of records. (The dub plates I use in performance are the only two that I have ever pressed.) But the acetate corrodes rapidly after continued contact with the oils and acids naturally found on human fingers, and so the two we use in our performances, cut in 2000, are nearing dissolution just ten years on, whereas vinyl would last indefinitely under the same conditions. I think of this impermanence as part of the performance, yet another echo of instability, mutability, and temporality.

Carried with the rest of our records, a dub plate of my poetry becomes one source among many in the performance. The effect, hopefully, demystifies authorship, estranges it, at least somewhat, from the Foucauldian "author function."[4] Early in the formation of the project, I intended to have my a cappella vocal of the poem conventionally pressed to vinyl rather than acetate dub plates, which would have meant a print run of at least a few hundred copies. (Conventional presses will not engage in the lengthy process of cutting vinyl unless they have an order in the hundreds or more.) I had wanted the dissemination of these records to extend the project, and to allow my voice/ poem to appear in multiple sites of performance, possibly beyond my knowing, in the work of other DJs and other artists of any sort. I eventually decided to use the one-off dub plates simply to save money, but the concept of vinyl is worth returning to. Nevertheless, even without the dissemination of the poem-record as a "ready-made" object, my vocal of the poem has appeared in the song "Yellow and Read" by Kentaro Ide (DJ Kentaro)—a reconstitution of my vocal artifact that was a welcome surprise and an intriguing re-contextualization. Ide uses some samples of the CD version of my poem in the midst of his hip hop composition that explores his mixed Asian-Canadian identity.[5]

My second stated goal was to subvert the trope of the common spoken-word performance, projected from the body, in favour of performance upon the art object. This repositioning of the author, I think, creates a different expression of agency. My mixed-race Afroeuropean body and de Couto's mixed-race Eurasian body both act by cueing, sampling, scratching, and equalizing the pre-recorded voice, rather than producing a unified semiotic meaning by direct address. In a society where the consumption of racialized bodies is a central part of the capitalist spectacle, consumers favour "authentic" racialized

creators. In this view, rappers and DJs are seen as less than artists, but instead as individuals who embody their culture intui-
tively and without meta-artistic consideration. (Hip hop music
has trended away from an age of political expression and commentary in the 1980s, when what individual lyricists thought
and believed mattered, to the current era in which a rapper's
proximity to the urban abject is his primary value.)[6] In our performance, we put the equipment in the foreground, between
ourselves and the audience, and we enact a commentary upon
it. My pre-recorded voice and poem is broken and re-broken,
arranged and re-arranged, combined and re-combined with a
shifting repertoire of other sources. Between us, the artists,
and you, the audience, is the material poem—on the tables,
under discussion, and subject to revision by the nature of the
performance's form. The poem is not inside me, waiting to be
expressed. It is in our crate, waiting for us to position it.

In his book *The Soundscape: Our Sonic Environment and
the Tuning of the World* (1993), R. Murray Schafer defines
the dislocation of the voice from the body through recording
technologies and electronic amplification as "schizophonia."
Schafer analyzes the various ways in which this phenomenon
pervades contemporary life. His view is generally negative,
and he asserts that schizophonia disrupts the natural flow of
life and breaks our connection to an ecologically contiguous
world. Following Schafer's criticism, it is interesting to note
that a live poetry reading is one space that is normally seen
as specifically defying schizophonia: a reading is meant to be
a chance to perceive the author's "genuine" presence. But dis-

rupting this pretense of naturalism seems to me like a useful tool—especially in a context where race and mixed-race are explicitly being addressed. Hip hop certainly has "elements" that have always decentralized the body and the "author": the illegality of graffiti art allows only pseudonymous fame; and turntablists always employ the art of others. But something that we could call—paraphrasing Foucault—the "MC function" has, nevertheless, become the central trope of hip hop, and one of the central commodities of the music industry. The denaturalization of this function offers a chance to dislocate false essentialisms of race and class that capital finds most easily marketable. Putting the art object at the centre, rather than the body in performance, and embracing schizophonia, can be liberating because it is unsettling.

My third experimental goal was to make each performance constitute a self-*détournement*—to be able to re-cast my own original poem in light of later dialectical turns. While the poem stays the same from performance to performance, and the vocal artifact is the same (the dub plate), it is with the paratactical placement of various found audio samples that the original poem acquires slight variations in meaning. For example, in a performance different from the one mentioned in the first part of this essay, we used three successive samples that each use a common image—the human hand. In this earlier performance, we also used the sample mentioned previously from the album *Alex Haley Tells the Story of His Search for Roots*. Whereas in our performance we compared Haley's traumatic epiphany of his own mixed-race with a general exploration of race as pareidolia, in this earlier performance, the auditory punctum, to borrow Roland Barthes' term[7] was, for me, Haley's emphasis on his hands at the moment of realization. He says, astonished: "I found myself studying my own hands. Inside, outside. And naturally it's in contrast to their complexions. [...] I felt hybrid. I felt impure among the pure." We lead off from this sample into one from my own poem, which reads:

> Up from my vestigial vinyl lobe, Blow
> at the conch shell goes, "These are the breaks."
> But these are the bends, on the real. Those gold
> chains at his throat—a rope alchemical and atrophied.
> When you were new school, we didn't know
> we would come to plunder your phatic calls to "Throw
> your hands in
> the air,"

> Kurtis. It is ridiculous to see this as anything but the down
> hill slope, sugar. My main
> man, my partner, my old school Prometheus,
> give me some skin in
> membrance. Finally
> it really is, we really are, I really am
> wavering
> like I just don't care. (2004, 107)

The sample from my poem was, in turn, book-ended by an excerpt from a CBC-recorded adaptation of Margaret Atwood's *The Journals of Susanna Moodie* (1970), read by actress Mia Anderson. In the Atwood sample, she describes Moodie's feeling that life in Canada is re-racializing her:

> [...] the sun here had stained
> me its barbarous colour
> Hands grown stiff, the fingers
> brittle as twigs
> eyes bewildered after
> seven years, and almost
> blind/buds, which can see
> only the wind
> the mouth cracking
> open like a rock in the fire
> trying to say
> What is this
> (you find only
> the shape you already are
> but what
> if you have forgotten that
> or discover you
> have never known)

Sampling provides the power of focus and re-contextualization: in Africa, Haley realizes his blackness is but a *version* of blackness while looking at his hands; in my lines I look at the rapper Kurtis Blow and the old-school, crowd-rousing line, "Throw your hands in the air," as an arbitrarily foundational moment which bleeds over into contemporary ambivalence; Atwood's Moodie re-perceives her whiteness, appropriating a variant of the *Bois-Brûlés* epithet, and she re-imagines her body browning in the colony. While my original lines did not anticipate the reading that appears within the context of these other depictions, it layers amongst them in the mix and becomes one among several transnational and transracial moments. In this way, we subvert my initial intention; intention erodes in the DJ-ing form. The echoing references to hands in each of the three samples also draws attention back to the material conditions of the performance, the dance of the hands over records and upfaders, the literal manipulation of sound and theme.

Against these poetical aspects of the performance, we also use music and noise to draw out concepts. As in the performance narrative above, de Couto's scratching is often used to comment on the spoken samples, and the choice of music can darken, lighten, or otherwise leaven the lexical meanings and sonically enjambed samples. While the bulk of the music we use is instrumental hip hop, we have also employed jazz, black spirituals, traditional Japanese music, and sound effects.

Thinking of Schafer in light of "The Reinventing Wheel," it is interesting to note that his negative definition of schizophonia is, at times in *The Soundscape*, associated with notions of race and nation. For example, he points out that the Nazis were among the earliest adopters of the loudspeaker, and he suggests that imperialism is a radiophonic ideology (1994, 91, 77). But I believe this is contradicted by the democratic presence of postmodern remix culture—which is perhaps best shown by Paul D. Miller (DJ Spooky that Subliminal Kid)'s landmark *Sound Unbound: Sampling, Digital Music and Culture* (2008), and is perhaps best described by Steven Feld's application of Gregory

Bateson's more neutral term "schismogenesis," the recombination of sounds split from their sources. Feld, unlike Schafer, emphasizes rupture as a creative act.[8] But we can be more partisan than that in our definitions of DJ culture and the commitment to sonic fragmentation. Our experiment, finally, might be called an example of "schizophonophilia": the love of audio interplay, the pleasure of critical disruptions to natural audition, the counter-hegemonic affirmation that can be achieved through acoustic intervention.

Whatever terms are used, the spirit of this particular performance experiment is embodied in the central instrument itself—the turntable—rather than the radio, the CD player, or the laptop computer. If we are celebrating the denaturalization of sound, there is no better tool than the phonograph, a Brechtian machine in its very making. Radios, CD players, and laptops are boxes—devices of enclosure—whereas the phonograph has always seemed to me to be a machine turned inside-out; a machine whose workings are always visible, whose interface is literally tangible, and whose production of sound is visceral. The body of a phonograph, like the body of a racialized object, can never close.

NOTES

1 This performance took place at the Scream in High Park Literary Festival, Toronto, Ontario, July 14, 2008.

2 "We are looking for the pedagogical arts of the contact zone. These will include, we are sure, exercises in storytelling and in identifying with the ideas, interests, histories, and attitudes of others; experiments in transculturation and collaborative work and in the arts of critique, parody, and comparison (including unseemly comparisons between elite and vernacular cultural forms); the redemption of the oral; ways for people to engage with suppressed aspects of history (including their own histories), ways to move into and out of rhetorics of authenticity; ground rules for communication across lines of difference and hierarchy that go beyond politeness but maintain mutual respect; a systematic approach to the all-important concept of cultural mediation." Mary Louise Pratt, "Arts of the Contact Zone," *Ways of Reading*, eds. David Bartholomae and Anthony Petrosky (Boston: Bedford-St. Martin's, 2002) 605–18.

3 Frantz Fanon, "On National Culture," *The Wretched of the Earth*, trans. Constance Farrington (New York: Grove, 1968) 206–48.

4 Michel Foucault, "What Is an Author?", *The Foucault Reader*, trans. Josué V. Harari, ed. Paul Rabinow (New York: Pantheon, 1984) 101–20.

5 Kentaro Ide, "Yellow and Read," personal home page, online audio file, n.d., July 18, 2008 <http://www.kreativity.spyw.com/>.

6 For an example of this kind of misreading of black artists as unthinkingly intuitive, see John Lennon's interview with Jann S. Wenner, "John Lennon: The Rolling Stone Interview, Part One: The Working Class Hero," *Rolling Stone* 74, January 21, 1971, www.jannswenner.com/Archives/John_Lennon_Part1.aspx: "The blues is real, it's not perverted or thought about, it's not a concept. It is a chair, not a design for a chair, or a better chair or a bigger chair or a chair with leather on … it is the first chair. It is a chair for sitting on, not for looking at or being appreciated. You *sit* on that music." It seems to me that Lennon's

kind of inability to recognize consideration, concept, and contrivance in blues music persists today in readings of all black art—from blues to jazz to hip hop to literature and to the visual arts.

7 Roland Barthes, *Camera Lucida: Reflections on Photography*, trans. Richard Howard (New York: Farrar, Straus and Giroux, 2000).

8 Steven Feld, "From Schizophonia to Schismogenisis: On the Discourses and Commodification Practices of 'World Music' and 'World Beat'" in *Music Grooves: Essays and Dialogues*, eds. Charles Keil and Steven Felt (Chicago: University of Chicago Press, 1994).

OBAMA AND LANGUAGE

"POST-RACE"

Three recent book titles feature this neologism:

> *Mixed-Race, Post-Race: Gender, New Ethnicities and Cultural Practices* (2005) by Suki Ali
>
> *The Construction and Rearticulation of Race in a 'Post-Racial America'* (2008) by Christopher J. Metzler
>
> *Racism in Post-Race America: New Theories, New Directions* (2008) by Charles A. Gallagher

The term "post-race" is clearly in use, and yet it remains under-defined. It elicits a knee-jerk disavowal. Race has vanished. But has racism vanished? Or is the connotation more subtle; our responses to racism have become hackneyed, but nuance may yet overtake the blunt instrument of identity politics. Use of the term expanded with Barack Obama's election campaign and presidency. But he is just a part of its constellation. Here is a walk through a few of my attempts to give "post-race" a definite sense.

In the popular press—at least in *Newsweek*—the term appears to mean that "race isn't supposed to matter anymore." It implies an era in which "everyone has 'gotten over' race" (Romano and Ammah-Tagoe, 2009). On right-wing American talk-radio, "post-race" means the disappearance of racism. An academic—Alana Lentin—uses the term negatively: "post-race" is a fallacy of triumphalist neoliberalism and white hegemony (2008, 90–93). Another—Brett St Louis—sees in the term a question of anti-racist tactics and asks, "How might a critical post-racial imagination that trades on the theoretical and conceptual bankruptcy of race and is committed to its erasure retain efficacy in a civil society and political culture largely arranged around its immense practical currency?" (2002, 661). It is the central contradiction of a transitional era. For yet others—Jo-Anne Lee and John Lutz—the word names a teleological dilemma—"Instead of seeing racism as 'the thing' to oppose, we need a clearly articulated vision of a post-racial world" (2005, 4). For them, "post-race" describes the revolutionary goal, which revolutionaries usually fail to depict while within the depths of struggle. Sociologist Suki Ali is loathe to reify the term and offsets it as "'post-race' thinking" or "'post-race' analysis" (2003, 8–9), lengthening the noun, as if this will keep the implications at bay. For Ali, it is best defined by Paul Gilroy—in *Against Race: Imagining Political Culture Beyond the Color Line* (2000)—where the term is not used at all. Gilroy says that strategic essentialism has run its course, that the argument against racism now needs to include an argument against the notion of race itself.

Are these the premises? The Obama phenomenon signals a need for ideological reconstruction; liberation strategies built upon race-as-real tilt toward authoritarianism, mysticism, collective self-flattery; the older models—Black Power, Afrocentrism, the late twentieth-century identity politics movements—are exhausted.

Obama has mainstreamed the criticism of strategic essentialism, but he is the evidence of change more than the changemaker. During the 2008 Democratic Party primary race, at least, his discourse seemed to signal a nuanced disengagement from race—one more subtle and textured than it has ever been at a mass media level.

The Jeremiah Wright controversy ("God damn America"—old model? exhausted?) was all black commonplaces: the undemocratic, aggressive, racist record of the United States.[1] Obama's "A More Perfect Union" speech distanced him from Wright, from these basics—disingenuously, surely, pragmatically, tactically—but more startlingly, it was Obama as a mixed-race subject that put him over, suggested a path of compromise for their nation.[2] The rhetorical turning point, the coalescence of a viable candidate, was co-created out of a refreshed sense of mixed race (after race?).

This Canadian/mixed/black/white witness views the spectacle and sees in Obama a US version of Pierre Elliott Trudeau—the youth cult, the charisma, the aura of a personality containing his nation's contradictions. In Trudeau's time—national unity; in the Obama phenomenon—the embodiment of a possible American answer to division. In this comparison, Obama's "A More Perfect Union" speech was Trudeau's 1968 St Jean-Baptiste Day parade, the one where separatists threw bottles and rocks at him and his entourage, and he refused to move, somehow never getting hit by the volleys, forming an instant media myth of a leader who might similarly *will* the nation through the social crisis.[3] It is sympathetic magic—electing leaders who seem to personify compromise, regardless of their actual policies and the material roots of the conflict—but there is the shape of truth within the illusionists' tricks. Both moments, Obama's speech and Trudeau's parade, were spectacular disavowals of their identification with perceived radicals of their own minority ethnic backgrounds. Obama's speech, and its remarkable polyvalence, suddenly made both American cable news *and* hip hop seem even clumsier in their handling of race than we already knew they were. An era of dispassionate consideration regarding identity seemed surprisingly at hand. Then he won. Then he ceased to speak about race. Then the backlash whipped the discourse back to 1961 standards—or thereabouts.[4]

"DOUBLE CONSCIOUSNESS"

W.E.B. DuBois laid it down—"double consciousness"—in *The Souls of Black Folk* (1903). Blacks in a white-supremacist society see themselves twice—once according to their own cultural values, and once according to the white eye. A cornerstone, a binary, oft revised and expanded. Tripled. Quadrupled. And more.[5] Along this critical line, one might call the audio recording of Obama's memoir *Dreams from My Father: A Story of Race and Inheritance* (1995) an example of "quadraphonic consciousness," if the oration—the physical voice—of its author can be used as a gauge of cultural perception. For while

Obama has been pitched as a bridging figure, a symmetrical subject who brings together black and white, his performative narration shows a consciousness that is obliged to inhabit multiple identity positions as a matter of course in his personal milieu: *multiple* black and *multiple* white focalizations, and even a hint of an internalized Asian consciousness.

Back to the right-wing reaction. After Obama gave a speech at a National Association for the Advancement of Colored People (NAACP) event, Rush Limbaugh said on his radio program that he "put on a fake accent" when talking to black audiences, and that this was a kind of reverse-racism ("Obama Disowns His Whiteness"). Attacks on Obama's "authenticity" are, predictably, confused, ludicrous; there is anxiety if he speaks black vernacular, there is anxiety if he does not. Limbaugh's presupposition is a monoracial norm. But can we not recuperate and claim linguistic drift as the "authentic" experience of one who moves in and out of cultural settings—one whose own family is a Venn diagram of ethnicities?

The drift is Obama's norm. Mine too. My poetics, too. My own acquired and strategic use of the black dialect is both contrived and natural—if natural means that it comes from a life that moves, changes, and passes in and out of blackness/whiteness. To make it yet more plain: black dialect is always created, is not static, is not perennially folksy. It moves and is moved by speaking agents.

As a text or time-based narration, Obama makes four voices out of his one within the first few *moments* of his memoir, enacting them in the narrative—

—his standard speech;

—the Kenyan English of his Aunt Jane, telephoning from Nairobi;

—the mid-western American twang of his maternal grand father;

—and his Kenyan father's speech, a "deep baritone" with a "British accent" (1995, 3–7).

Not just the voices of these characters, but the auditory memories, the imprint upon the author's voice, the author's persona. (Obama's standard speech, the bulk of his talking, sounds to my ears most like his grandfather's, with something else—a regional Hawaiian tone?—lacing it.)

And more: when the author/speaker is four years old and his mother marries Lolo Soetoro, an Indonesian student, Obama narrates long passages of dialogue in which his stepfather teaches him lessons about power. The performance of Soetoro's English by Obama is that of a stern, staccato, masculine rap. Soetoro tells the author, a boy at the time, that a man he saw killed once was "weak" and that, "If you can't be strong, be clever and make peace with someone who's strong. But always better to be strong yourself. Always" (40–41). One hears Obama thinking through the implications as he speaks Soetoro's stoicism. Inflection is part of his process of internalizing and evaluating this bleak ethic.

And still more: when the adolescent Obama, back in Hawaii, meets the character Ray, we hear black American English as Obama first heard it—and tentatively employed it—during discussions that were themselves about "authenticity." He says to

Ray, "Maybe we could afford to give the bad-assed nigger pose a rest," taking "the dozens" a little too far. Ray answers, "A pose, huh? Speak for your own self" (82). And thereafter, during the author's sojourns through ideological Black Power and community organizing, his acquired black vernacular seems just a part of a personal pidgin—a bend of a vowel here, the use of a term there, a way of thinking the words into selfhood. By the time Limbaugh heard him talking before the NAACP in 2008, the weight of a long, lived journey was behind Obama's hybrid voice.

In the same screed, Limbaugh sees reverse-racism in every reference to black dissatisfaction that Obama names. Limbaugh believes that simply speaking about anti-black racism opens "race wounds" and "take[s] us back 30, 40 years, making it look like no progress has been made." He positively cites a previous time, when "Barack Obama had succeeded in transcending race […] He was smart, well-spoken. He was competent. He was able to excite crowds. He looked young and fresh and new. Furthermore, he was black, but it didn't matter to him." To speak of racism causes racism, Limbaugh asserts. Racelessness is progress. Never speaking of race is racelessness.

But the real transcendence is neither this denial nor Obama as merely the final assuagement of a black-white conflict, a symbolic embodiment of demographic compromise. It is the fluidity of identity that is the memoir's finest theme, the assertion of an unstationary consciousness, a system of identification that can move into positions beyond the fables of perceptual solidity.

"HALFRICAN"

In 2009 I noticed that someone had added to the biographical note on my Wikipedia page the following sentence: "In 1996 he penned the semi-autobiographical poem 'Declaration of the Halfrican Nation.'" Why this *particular* poem, of all that I have published, should be singularly mentioned was a mystery: it is not my best poem; it is not more frequently anthologized than any of my other poems. But I also noticed that within the title of the poem, the word "Halfrican" linked to a page of its own. I clicked it.

The Wikipedia page for the word "Halfrican" says, awkwardly, that "it is a possibly pejorative term used to refer to a person of both Black African and White European ancestry."[6] And the page compiles a list of people who have used the term publicly—

—2008, Julie Banderas, referring to Barack Obama.

—2007, Rush Limbaugh, referring to Halle Berry and Barack Obama.

—2006, Brian Sussman, referring to Barack Obama.

—1998, Jeff Rogers, referring to himself.

—1996, Wayde Compton, referring to himself.

Banderas is a television correspondent, Limbaugh and Sussman are both radio show hosts, Rogers was a teenager at the time he recorded a National Public Radio show in which he speaks about his own racialized experience. According to this page, I appear to be the coiner of the term.

So I searched the web for my name, the word "halfrican," and reference to these controversial usages. What poured forth was a strange trail of blogger rants and flame wars, some of which rested upon *my* use of the term as evidence that it either is or is not racist. Three examples:

1. Chip Bennett, in a blog entry defending Limbaugh against the charge that his use of the term was racist: "However, context really is irrelevant in this case. The term 'Halfrican American' was coined over a decade ago in a poem by Wayde Compton, is used as a self-description by bi-racial persons, and has no derogatory connotation whatsoever (unless one wants to make the absurd claim that *Urban Dictionary* is racist against black people). 'Halfrican' and 'Halfrican-American' are simply not considered to be racially derogatory by those to whom the term applies (and there certainly exist many such derogatory terms for biracial persons)."

2. "Indep1," someone's web identity, commenting on an article, inarticulately echoes Bennett's argument:

> [...] I'm man enough to look at a question you raised.
>
> Lets [sic] look at "Just because you referred to Barack Obama and Halle Berry as "Halfrican Americans?" This was allegedly said in a humor intro to a show segment. The problem that you, Pitts, and others may have is a lack of familiarity with the term "Halfrican". Because the term is perhaps unknown to you or other readers, you assign your private interpretation to it. I suggest that some homework is in order.
>
> The term "Halfrican" was coined by Canadian writer Wade [sic] Compton in his 1996 book [sic] entitled

"Declaration of the Halfrican Nation". It is certainly not a pejorative term or a term of ridicule. Why don't you look up "halfrican" or "halfrican American" in the *Urban Dictionary* and see what it says. Then report back and tell us if it is an insulting term. it [sic] is certainly more acceptable than the dated term "mulatto".

3. "James Davidson," commenting on an article titled, "The Lucrative Business of Racism," writes:

1. If you consider "Magic Negro" [a novelty song mocking Obama] offensive, and I do, note that it started on the Left: "Obama the 'Magic Negro': The Illinois senator lends himself to white America's idealized, less-than-real black man." By David Ehrenstein [...]

2. If you consider the Obama-Joker poster offensive, and I do, note that it also started on the Left [...]

3. "Halfrican" is a closer call, and whther [sic] it is offensive depends on intent, but it seems to have started in poetry, "Declaration of the Halfrican Nation," Wayde Compton (1996). Compton himself is Canadian and biracial.

And so forth.

Bennett, of course, has it perfectly backwards—context is everything. Banderas uses it confusedly. In answer to the question "Do minorities hate other minorities?," she says, "[Obama's] a Halfrican anyway, so I'm not really quite sure why the Asians and the Hispanics have no—you know, have a problem with him"—meaning, because he is only half black, other minorities should not consider him black. Limbaugh uses it to imply that Obama primarily has the support of mixed people, and not black voters who do not consider themselves mixed: "Hey, Barack Obama has picked up another endorsement: Halfrican American actress Halle Berry. 'As a Halfrican American, I am honored to have Ms. Berry's support, as well as the support of other Halfrican Americans,' Obama said. He didn't say it, but—anyway, there are those out there—greetings" ("Limbaugh on Obama: Halfrican American"). Sussman, answering a lead-in that runs "Senator Obama, who is, as you call [him], a 'Halfrican,'" says,

> Halfrican and, again, his father was—his father was
> from Kenya, his mother's white. OK, now, I have noth-
> ing with mixed—nothing against mixed-race people
> but, my point is, when this guy stands in front of a
> black audience, pretending like he was born and raised
> in the 'hood, and he can identify with their problems,
> he doesn't allow—he is not, in my opinion—'cause my
> opinion is your average white guy—he is not allowed to
> wear the African American badge because his family are
> not the descendants of slaves, OK? He can't identify with
> the discrimination and the slavery and all of that that's
> gone into these black families for generations; he's a kid
> who was raised with a silver spoon in his mouth in a
> white family in Hawaii, OK? You wanna call me names
> for saying this? Go right ahead. I'm just telling you what
> the guy is.

This makes it clear that Sussman is using the term to denote a black identity position that is "inauthentic" by virtue of being derived from experiences other than slavery and poverty. Rogers, conversely, uses the term to position his racialized experience growing up in Boston; to normalize something that others imply is abnormal:

> Usually when someone asks what I am, I say I'm halfrican. You know, my father's black, my mother's white, and when I was younger, to me that was the way it was supposed to be. Father meant black person. Mother meant white person. You know? I thought, to me it was normal. [...] It's like they always had the argument nature versus nurture. You know? Is it the way you're brought up or just the way you're born? When you're younger, you don't ponder, you know, Who am I? What, what, why am I here? You know? You're just living for the day. Having fun, watching *Teenage Mutant Ninja Turtles*, and eating cereal. Then, you know you hit that beautiful certain age, and you start to redefine yourself.

And my poem in full:

"Declaration of the Halfrican Nation"

hazel's so definitive. is the window
half open or half closed? is a black
rose natural? is it indigenous to this
coast? my grammar teacher said a semi-
colon is just a gutless colon; yellow. co-
conuts get eaten from the inside, the sweetness

and light from the milk and the flesh, not
the husk, so skull-like. one
friend said she's white except
for having this brown skin and sometimes she forgets it until a mirror shatters
that conclusion casting blackward glances side-
ways, askance processions of belonging, possession. mirrors
  walk
on two legs too sometimes, saying hello to you cause
you are brown
as we pass. what is britannia
to me? one three continents removed
from the scenes my mothers loved,
misty grove, english rose,
what is britannia to me?
ain't no negroes on the tv shows we
produced in playground theatres; now
there's so many on screen a white acquaintance of mine
thought the us population was half
black! one drop rules aside and all
things being equal, I'd say that signifies
an inexorable triumph of mlk's dream. we number a dozen percent, in fact, south
of the border; in canada, I really couldn't
begin to guess our numbers crunching
through the snow on shoes of woven
koya. black hippies; black punk rockers;
black goths with white masks *literally*
multiply like flesh-eating bacteria on the west coast. racism
is a disease, the ministry decrees to me in my bus seat
from an ad, and I could add
that this is just the latest stage in race management. canada

all
in a rush to recruit more brown whites; entrepreneurs only, no more slaves or railroad builders,
iron chinks or tempered niggers. the wages
of empire have yet to be spilled. oka. all
I halfta do is spell it and the settled snow shivers. one settler,
one bullet, south africans sang, palestinians sing; the tune
is boomin. is the mention
of bullets too american? the best way
anyone ever referred to me as mixed-race was a jamaican
woman who said, *I notice you're touched.* to
me sounded like she meant by the hand of god
(or the god of hands), and not the tar brush. made me
feel like a motherless child a long, long way
from my home. feel like history got me
by the throat. sometimes I feel like frantz fanon's ghost
is kickin back with a coke and rum having
a good chuckle at all this, stirring in the tears, his work
done, lounging with the spirits. oh, all
my fellow mixed sisters and brothers let us mount
an offensive for our state. surely something
can be put together from the tracts, manifestoes, auto-
biographies, ten point programs, constitutions, and historical
claims. I know more than enough who've ex-
pressed an interest in dying on the wire just for the victory
of being an agreed-upon proper noun (1996, 8–11)

Like Rogers, this is my experience, but in relief against my
local demographics and Canadian multicultural policy, trem-
bling, it seems to me now, with anxieties about how to recon-
cile marginality with public perceptions. I wrote this when I

was only twenty-four years old. The term "halfrican," as I use it, is facetious, a satirical tonic for the problem of a disunified identity. The tone is ironic, and the term is positioned as the emblem of the desire for recognition, representation, and cultural clarity. At the time, I wanted both the ease of identity that monoracial people seem to have, yet distrusted it as a false goal. Today, I would go further and advocate a more specific defence of racial complication.[7]

Context is all.

Banderas, Limbaugh, and Sussman are searching, with this term, for a way to publicly attack the heteroracial as false, unreal. For them, it is an epithet; like most epithets, it is strangely devoid of inherent derogatory denotation. Think "nigger," "chink," "spic"—etymologically empty. We know what is meant by them. But they are derogatory, one realizes, only because they are intentional misspeakings. The epithet lives in the intention to say the *neutral* racial term wrongly: "Negro," "Chinese," "Hispanic." If "halfrican" is such a purposeful misinvocation, it is a slur; if it is a self-invocation, it can be nothing less than a way out—

A MORE PERFECT IRREDUCIBILITY

—and back into the Obama phenomenon. Rather than a unifying compromise, perhaps the promise of the age, post-racial or not, is the hope and change of unapologetic complexity. Rather than new unities, solid identities, and centralized blackness, the future will be a time of identity in motion. As progressive as the moment seemed—that Obama was able to campaign

and win upon a relatively subtle argument from double consciousness—inside the executive position he has become mute
on identity. The centralization of the argument—two solitudes
(in US form), black and white, coupled in the person of the head
of state—has actually blunted the dialogue and allowed old-
model racism to assume a rebel pose. The value to be gained,
the lesson learned, seems to be the vibrancy of remaining outside the power—to speak against, perhaps, is the only way to
speak at all of race—after, or not—and into lasting liberation.

NOTES

1 Brian Ross and Rehab El-Buri, "Obama's Pastor: God Damn America, US to Blame for 9/11," *ABC News,* March 13, 2008, March 11, 2010 <http://abcnews.go.com/Blotter/DemocraticDebate/story?id=4443788&page=1>.

2 Barack Obama, "A More Perfect Union," online video, *YouTube,* March 18, 2008, March 11, 2010 <http://www.youtube.com/watch?v=zrp-v2tHaDo>.

3 "The PM won't let 'em rain on his parade," *CBC Digital Archives*, June 24, 1968, August 31, 2009 <http://archives.cbc.ca/politics/prime_ministers/topics/2192-13270/>.

4 For a detailed and raucous discussion of the right-wing reaction to Obama, see Ishmael Reed, *Barack Obama and the Jim Crow Media: The Return of the Nigger Breakers* (Montréal: Baraka, 2010).

5 "[T]he African-Canadian consciousness is not simply dualistic. We are divided severally; we are not just 'black' and Canadian, but also adherents to a region, speakers of an 'official' language (either English or French), disciples of heterogeneous faiths, and related to a particular ethnicity (or 'national' group), all of which shapes our identities. African Canadians possess, then, not merely 'double consciousness' but what I will call poly-consciousness." George Elliott Clarke, "Contesting a Model Blackness: A Meditation on African-Canadian African-Americanism, or the Structures of African-Canadianité," in Clarke, *Odysseys Home: Mapping African-Canadian Literature* (Toronto: University of Toronto Press, 2002), 40.

6 During the last stages of editing this essay, the Wikipedia page for the term "Halfrican" was removed altogether, and the link from the "Wayde Compton" page was instead directed to a Wiktionary entry that excludes much of the information quoted here. (See "Halfrican," *Wiktionary: The Free Dictionary*, Wikimedia Foundation, January 6, 2010, March 11, 2010 <http://en.wiktionary.org/wiki/Halfrican>.) Nevertheless, the history of the page is still available, at the moment I write this, at "Revision history of Halfrican," *Wikipedia: The Free*

Encyclopedia, Wikimedia Foundation, March 19, 2008, March 7, 2010, March 11, 2010 <http://en.wikipedia.org/w/index.php?title=Hal frican&action=history>.

7 For the most complete reading of this poem to date, see George Elliott Clarke, "Canadian Biraciality and Its 'Zebra' Poetics," *Odysseys Home: Mapping African-Canadian Literature* (Toronto: University of Toronto Press, 2002) 211–37.

WORKS CITED

2006 Community Profiles: Vancouver: Visible Minority Population Characteristics, *Statistics Canada*, February 5, 2010. http://
www12.statcan.ca/census-recensement/2006/dp-pd/prof/92-591/
details/page.cfm?Lang=E&Geo1=CMA&Code1=933__&Geo2=P
R&Code2=59&Data=Count&SearchText=Vancouver&SearchTyp
e=Begins&SearchPR=01&B1=Visible%20minority&Custom= (accessed March 22, 2010).

Adair, Robin. Letter. *Cariboo Sentinel*, supplement, July 29, 1865.

Ali, Suki. *Mixed-Race, Post-Race: Gender, New Ethnicities and
Cultural Practices*. Oxford, UK: Berg, 2003.

Atkin, John. *Strathcona: Vancouver's First Neighbourhood*. North
Vancouver: Whitecap, 1994.

Atwood, Margaret. *The Journals of Susanna Moodie*. LP. Read by
Mia Anderson. Canadian Broadcasting Corporation, 1971.

Barthes, Roland. *Camera Lucida: Reflections on Photography*.
Translated by Richard Howard. New York: Farrar, Straus, and
Giroux, 2000.

Baumeister, Roy F., and Brad J. Bushman. *Social Psychology and Human Nature*, 2nd ed. Belmont, CA: Wadsworth, 2010.

Bennett, Chip. "Debunking Alleged Racist Limbaugh Quotes."
CB.Blog. Weblog entry, October 24, 2009. http://www.chipben-
nett.net/wordpress/2009/10/debunking-alleged-racist-limbaugh-
quotes/ (accessed March 11, 2010).

Book, Shane. "Border Crossings." *Geist* 8, no. 34 (1999): 24–27.

Booker, Fred. *Adventures in Debt Collection*. Vancouver: Commodore, 2006.

———. *Dear Jane: Book Three*. Rulebook Records, 1978.

————. "From 'Blue Notes of a White Girl'." In *Bluesprint: Black British Columbian Literature and Orature*, edited by Wayde Compton. Vancouver: Arsenal Pulp, 2001. 136–46.

————. "A Review: *John Ware's Cow Country*." *Canadian Dimension* 14, no. 1 (July–August 1979): 49–51.

————. "Three selections from 'In Spaces We Live'." *Prism International* 22, no. 4 (July 1984): 68–70.

Boom Bip. "Awaiting an Accident." *Seed to Sun*. LP. London: Lex, 2002.

British Colonist. "Rise of the Curtain on the Municipal Candidates." August 12, 1862.

Brown, Rosemary. *Being Brown: A Very Public Life*. Toronto: Random House, 1989.

Burns, Robert. "To a Louse." In *The Norton Anthology of English Literature*. 5th ed., edited by M.H. Abrams et al., vol. 2: 93–94. New York and London: W.W. Norton, 1986.

Carleton, J. Harry. "Bones in Love." In *Minstrel Gags and End Men's Hand-Book*. New York: Dick and Fitzgerald, n.d.

"Chilling Out." *Everyman* series, DVD. Produced by Lucy Parker. London: BBC One Television, broadcast February 25, 1990.

"Canada's Poorest Postal Code." Weblog comment. "V6A: No condo for this postal code." Weblog entry. *Condohype: Vancouver: Disown the Lifestyle*, October 24, 2008. http://condohype.wordpress.com/2008/10/24/v6a-no-condo-for-this-postal-code/ (accessed October 25, 2008).

Clarke, George Elliott. "Canadian Biraciality and Its 'Zebra' Poetics." In *Odysseys Home: Mapping African-Canadian Literature*, 211–37. Toronto: University of Toronto Press, 2002.

Compton, Wayde, ed. *Bluesprint: Black British Columbian Literature and Orature.* Vancouver: Arsenal Pulp Press, 2001.

———. *Performance Bond.* Vancouver: Arsenal Pulp Press, 2004.

———. "Declaration of the Halfrican Nation." *Absinthe* 9, no. 2 (1996): 8–11. Reprinted in *Performance Bond*, 15–16.

Coupland, Douglas. *City of Glass: Douglas Coupland's Vancouver.* Vancouver: Douglas and McIntyre, 2003.

Davidson, James. "If you consider ..." Website comment on Bob Weir, "The Lucrative Business of Racism." *Real Clear Politics*, October 19, 2009. http://comments.realclearpolitics.com/read.php?1,477229,477521,quote= (accessed on March 11, 2010).

The Dead Dog Café Comedy Hour. CBC Radio One. 1997–2000.

"The Decommissioning of 823 Jackson Avenue, Once the African Methodist Episcopal Fountain Chapel." Weblog entry, *Hogan's Alley Memorial Project: Memorializing Vancouver's Historic Black Neighbourhood and the Wider Vancouver Black Experience*, November 1, 2008. http://hogansalleyproject.blogspot.com/2008/11/on-26-october-2008-basel-hakka-lutheran.html (accessed March 4, 2010).

Digable Planets. "Dial 7 (Axioms of Creamy Spies) (Instrumental)." *Dial 7/Graffiti.* LP. Pendulum, 1995.

Dixie (Isaac Dickson). Letter. *Cariboo Sentinel*, supplement, June 12, 1865 (1865a). In *Bluesprint: Black British Columbian Literature and Orature,* edited by Wayde Compton, 65–6. Vancouver: Arsenal Pulp Press, 2001.

———. Letter. Cariboo Sentinel, supplement, July 1, 1865 (1865b). In *Bluesprint: Black British Columbian Literature and Orature*, 67–8.

DJ Krush and Toshinori Kondo. "Ha-doh." *Ki-oku*. LP. Instinct, 1999.

DJ Qbert. *Secret of the Y Formula*. LP. Thud Rumble, 2001.

Dreisinger, Baz. *Near Black: White-to-Black Passing in American Culture*. Amherst, MA: University of Massachusetts Press, 2008.

Dubois, W.E.B. *The Souls of Black Folk*. 1903. Project Gutenberg, 2008.http://www.gutenberg.org/files/408/408-h/408-h.htm (accessed March 11, 2010).

Dunning, Brian. "When People Talk Backwards." *Skeptoid: Critical Analysis Podcast* 105 (June 17, 2008). http://skeptoid.com/episodes/4105 (accessed July 18, 2008).

Engstrom, Mark D. "Re: 'pheneticizing'." Email to the author. April 12, 2010.

Fanon, Frantz. "On National Culture." *The Wretched of the Earth*. Translated by Constance Farrington. New York: Grove, 1968. 206-48.

Feld, Steven. "From Schizophonia to Schismogenesis: On the Discourses and Commodification Practices of 'World Music' and 'World Beat'." In *Music Grooves: Essays and Dialogues*, edited by Charles Keil and Steven Feld. Chicago: University of Chicago Press, 1994.

Fix: The Story of an Addicted City. DVD. Dir. Nettie Wild. Canada Wild Productions, 2002.

Foucault, Michel. "What Is an Author?" Translated by Josué V. Harari. In *The Foucault Reader*, edited by Paul Rabinow. New York: Pantheon, 1984. 101–20.

"Fox News host Banderas called Obama a 'Halfrican.'" *Media Matters*, February 13, 2008. http://mediamatters.org/mmtv/200802130014 (accessed March 11, 2010).

Gallagher, Charles A. *Racism in Post-Race America: New Theories, New Directions*. Chapel Hill, NC: Social Forces, 2008.

Gates, Henry Louis. "The Trope of the Talking Book." In *Criticism: Major Statements*, edited by Charles Kaplan and William Anderson. New York: St. Martin's, 1991, 778–830.

Gibbs, Mifflin Wistar. *Shadow and Light: An Autobiography with Reminiscences of the Last and Present Century*. Lincoln, NB: University of Nebraska Press, 1995.

Gilroy, Paul. *Against Race: Imagining Political Culture Beyond the Color Line*. Cambridge, MA: Belknap, 2000.

———. *The Black Atlantic: Modernity and Double Consciousness*. Cambridge, MA: Harvard University Press, 1995.

Government of Alberta. "The Legend of John Ware." *Alberta Centennial*, 2002. http://www.albertacentennial.ca/history/viewpost.aspx~id=245.html (accessed June 21, 2008).

Griffin, Kevin C. *Vancouver's Many Faces: Passport to the Cultures of a City*. North Vancouver: Whitecap, 1993.

guardian.co.uk. "Behavioural biology expert puts forward theory of why we laugh." June 4, 2009. http://www.guardian.co.uk/science/2009/jun/04/why-laughter-behavioural-biology (accessed March 5, 2010).

"Guerrilla art and public memory." Weblog entry. *Hogan's Alley Memorial Project: Memorializing Vancouver's Historic Black Neighbourhood and the Wider Vancouver Black Experience*, July 9, 2007. http://hogansalleyproject.blogspot.com/2007_07_01_archive.html (accessed August 1, 2009).

Haley, Alex. *Alex Haley Tells the Story of His Search for Roots*. LP. Burbank, CA: Warner Bros., 1977.

Harcourt, Mike and Ken Cameron. *City Making in Paradise: Nine*

Decisions That Saved Vancouver. Vancouver: Douglas and Mc-Intyre, 2007.

Harrison, Guy P. *Race and Reality: What Everyone Should Know about Our Biological Diversity*. Buffalo, NY: Prometheus, 2009.

Hauka, Donald J. *McGowan's War*. Vancouver: New Star, 2003.

Hendrix, James A. and Jas Obrecht. *My Son Jimi*. Seattle: Aljas Enterprises, 1999.

Hendrix, Nora. Interview with Daphne Marlatt and Carole Itter. In *Opening Doors: Vancouver's East End*, edited by Daphne Marlatt and Carole Itter. Victoria: Province of BC, Provincial Archives, 1979.

Hogan's Alley. VHS. Directed by Andrea Fatona and Cornelia Wyngaarden. Video Out, 1994.

"Hogan's Alley Before the Demolition." City of Vancouver Archives, July 16, 2009, http://vancouver.ca/ctyclerk/archives/exhibits/HogansAlley/index.htm (accessed August 1, 2009).

Howard, Irene. *The Struggle for Social Justice in British Columbia: Helena Gutteridge, the Unknown Reformer*. Vancouver: University of British Columbia Press, 1992.

Hudson, Peter. Editorial. "Diaspora: The Cap Review Remix." Special issue of *Capilano Review* 2, no. 33 (Winter 2001).

———. "Natural Histories of Southwestern British Columbia." The Sitelines Issue. Special issue, *West Coast LINE* 31.3, no. 24 (Winter 1997–98): 19–22.

Ide, Kentaro. "Yellow and Read." Home page. Online audio file. http://www.kreativity.spyw.com/ (accessed July 18, 2008; site now discontinued).

Indep1. "Casablanca, the reason …" Website comment on Leonard Pitts Jr., "Searching for a reason to rally around Rush Limbaugh."

Cleveland.com, October 24, 2009. http://www.cleveland.com/
opinion/index.ssf/2009/10/searching_for_a_reason_to_rall/4702/
comments-newest.html (accessed March 11, 2010).

Jacobs, Jane. *The Death and Life of Great American Cities*. 1961.
New York: Vintage, 1992.

The Kids in the Hall. CBC. 1988–94. Television series.

Kilian, Crawford. *Go Do Some Great Thing: The Black Pioneers of
British Columbia*. Burnaby, BC: Commodore, 2008.

Lambertson, Ross. "The Black, Brown, White and Red Blues: The
Beating of Clarence Clemons." *Canadian Historical Review* 85,
no. 4 (December 2004): 755–76.

Lee, Joanne and John Lutz. "Introduction: Toward a Critical Literacy
of Racisms, Anti-Racisms, and Racialization." *Situating "Race"
and Racisms in Space, Time and Theory: Critical Essays for Activists and Scholars*. Edited by Joanne Lee and John Lutz. Montreal
and Kingston: McGill-Queen's University Press, 2005.

Lentin, Alana. *Racism: A Beginner's Guide*. Oxford, UK: Oneworld,
2008.

Limbaugh, Rush. "Obama Disowns His Whiteness." Transcribed
radio show. *The Rush Limbaugh Show*, March 21, 2008.
http://www.rushlimbaugh.com/home/daily/site_032108/con-
tent/01125111.html (accessed August 31, 2009).

"Limbaugh on Obama: Halfrican American." *Media Matters*, January 24, 2007. http://mediamatters.org/research/200701240010
(accessed March 11, 2010).

Live Human. "Eggroll Suite." *Elefish Jellyphant*. LP. New York:
Matador, 2000.

Long Lance, Chief Buffalo Child. *Long Lance: The Autobiography
of a Blackfoot Indian Chief*. London: Faber and Faber, 1956.

Longfellow, Henry Wadsworth. *The Song of Hiawatha*. 1855. Charlottesville: Electronic Text Center, University of Virginia Library, 2000. http://etext.lib.virginia.edu/toc/modeng/public/LonHiaw.html (accessed March 4, 2010).

Macdonald, Bruce. *Vancouver: A Visual History*. Vancouver: Talonbooks, 1992.

MacLean, Alyssa. "Rough Crossings: Considering Lake Erie as a Site on the Black Atlantic." Unpublished paper presented at the "Culture and the Canada-US Border" conference, Canterbury, UK, 2009.

Marlatt, Daphne and Carole Itter, eds. *Opening Doors: Vancouver's East End*. Victoria: Province of BC, Provincial Archives, 1979.

Marsden, Lauren. "Hogan's Alley Welcomes You." Lauren Marsden, personal home page. July 2007. http://www.laurenmarsden.com/imagepages/images_hogans.html (accessed August 1, 2009, page discontinued).

Marsh, Leonard. *Rebuilding a Neighbourhood: Report on a Demonstration Slum-Clearance and Urban Rehabilitation Project in a Key Central Area in Vancouver*. Vancouver: University of British Columbia, 1950.

Mayne, R.C. *Four Years in British Columbia and Vancouver Island*. London: John Murray, 1862.

McCardell, Mike. "Three Stories from the DTES with Mike McCardell." *Vancouver Province*, February 8, 2009. http://www.theprovince.com/news/Three+stories+from+DTES+with+Mike+McCardell/1260701/story.html (accessed August 1, 2009, page discontinued).

McKellar, Keith. "Vie's Chicken and Steak House." *Neon Eulogy: Vancouver Cafe and Street*. Victoria: Ekstasis, 2001. 83–85.

"Melanie Morgan co-host on 'Halfrican' Obama." *Media Matters*, December 7, 2006. http://mediamatters.org/research/200612070006 (accessed March 11, 2010).

Metzler, Christopher J. *The Construction and Rearticulation of Race in a 'Post-Racial America.'* Bloomington, IN: AuthorHouse, 2008.

"Militant Mothers of Raymur." Weblog entry. *Viaduct: Travels Through East Vancouver*, June 25, 2008. http://viaducteast.ca/2008/06/25/militant-mothers-of-raymur/ (accessed August 1, 2009).

Miller, Paul D. and Steve Reich, eds. *Sound Unbound: Sampling, Digital Music and Culture*. Cambridge, MA: MIT Press, 2008.

Mollineaux, Melinda. "Cadboro Bay Photographs." *The Capilano Review* 2, no. 29 (Fall 1999): 47–56.

"Mr. Taharka Anthony Lennon Ekundayo." Hogarth Blake. 2009. http://www.hh-bb.com/taharka-ekundayo.html (accessed July 30, 2009).

Nealy, Dorothy. Interview with Daphne Marlatt and Carole Itter. *Opening Doors: Vancouver's East End*. Eds. Daphne Marlatt and Carole Itter. Victoria: Province of BC, Provincial Archives, 1979. 169–74.

Obama, Barack. *Dreams from My Father: A Story of Race and Inheritance*. 1995. New York: Three Rivers, 2004.

The Office. "Diversity Day." Episode 1-02, first broadcast March 29, 2005, by NBC. Directed by Ken Kwapis and written by B.J. Novak.

Oxford English Dictionary Online. Oxford University Press, 2010. http://dictionary.oed.com/

Paulsen, Monte. "Vancouver Election Spending Out of Control." *The Tyee*, October 31, 2007. http://thetyee.ca/News/2007/10/31/CityCampaignDollars/ (accessed August 1, 2009).

Pilton, James W. "Negro Settlement in British Columbia, 1858–1871." M.A. thesis, University of British Columbia, 1951.

"The PM won't let 'em rain on his parade." Online video. CBC Digital Archives, June 24, 1968. http://archives.cbc.ca/politics/prime_ministers/topics/2192-13270/ (accessed August 31, 2009).

Pratt, Mary Louise. "Arts of the Contact Zone." In *Ways of Reading*, edited by David Bartholomae and Anthony Petrosky. Boston: Bedford-St. Martin's, 2002. 605–18.

"Province investigating condo developer Onni." CTV British Columbia, October 24, 2008. http://www.ctvbc.ctv.ca/servlet/an/local/CTVNews/20081024/BC_condos_real_estate_081024/20081024/?hub=BritishColumbiaHome (accessed October 25, 2008).

Pryor, Richard. *Live and Smokin'*. VHS. Directed by Michael Blum. 1971; Chicago: MPI Home Video, 1985.

———. *Live in Concert*. DVD. Directed by Jeff Margolis. 1979; Chicago: MPI Home Video, 1998.

———. *That Nigger's Crazy*. Audiocassette. 1974; Burbank, CA: Warner Bros., 1990.

Punter, John. *The Vancouver Achievement: Urban Planning and Design*. Vancouver: University of British Columbia Press, 2003.

Ramsey, Bruce. "Negroes Live Next Door." *Vancouver Sun* (July 19, 1952): 15.

———. "Vancouver's first lifeguard: Remembering the days of 'Old Black Joe.'" *Vancouver Province*, March 16, 1964, final ed.

Reed, Ishmael. *Barack Obama and the Jim Crow Media: The Return of the Nigger Breakers*. Montreal: Baraka, 2010.

The Road Taken. DVD. Directed by Selwyn Jacob. National Film Board of Canada, 1996.

Rock, Chris. *Bring the Pain*. Directed by Keith Truesdell. 1996; Universal City, CA: Dreamworks, 2002.

Rogers, Jeff. "Halfrican." *National Public Radio: All Thing Considered*. Produced by Joe Richman. Radio Diaries. Transcript. November 13, 1998. http://www.radiodiaries.org/transcripts/TeenageDiaries/Jeff.html (accessed March 11, 2010).

Romano, Andrew and Aku Ammah-Tagoe. "Black in the Age of Obama." *Newsweek*, April 18, 2009. http://www.newsweek.com/id/194592 (accessed March 10, 2010, page discontinued).

Russwurm, Lani. "The Elusive Hogan's Alley, Part 2." Weblog entry. *Past Tense: Fragments of Vancouver History and Reflections Thereon*, April 5, 2008. http://pasttensevancouver.wordpress.com/2008/04/05/the-elusive-hogans-alley-part-2/ (accessed August 1, 2009).

Schafer, R. Murray. *The Soundscape: Our Sonic Environment and the Tuning of the World*. Rochester, VT: Destiny, 1994.

Shepherd, Bruce R. *Deemed Unsuitable: Blacks from Oklahoma Move to the Canadian Prairies in Search of Equality in the Early 20th Century Only to Find Racism in Their New Home*. Toronto: Umbrella, 1997.

Smith, Charleen P. "Boomtown Brothels in the Kootenays, 1895–1905." In *People and Place: Historical Influences of Legal Culture*, edited by Jonathan Swainger and Constance Backhouse. Vancouver: University of British Columbia Press, 2004.

Smith, Donald B. *Chief Buffalo Child Long Lance: The Glorious Impostor*. Red Deer, AB: Red Deer Press, 1999.

Snyders, Tom and Jennifer O'Rourke. *Namely Vancouver: A Hidden History of Vancouver Place Names*. Vancouver: Arsenal Pulp, 2002.

Stepler, Jack. "Hogan's Alley Fate at Stake." *Vancouver Daily Province*, April 21, 1939.

St Louis, Brett. "Post-race/post-politics? Activist-intellectualism and the reification of race." *Ethnic and Racial Studies* 25, no. 4 (July 2002): 652–75.

"Study shows Downtown Eastside housing situation is getting worse." Weblog entry. *Carnegie Community Action Project,* June 17, 2009.http://ccapvancouver.wordpress.com/2009/06/17/study-shows-downtown-eastside-housing-situation-is-getting-worse/ (accessed August 1, 2009).

A Tribe of One. DVD. Directed by Eunhee Cha. Montreal: National Film Board of Canada, 2003.

Urbaniak, Michał. "Atma." *Fusion*. LP. Columbia, 1974.

"V6A." Advertisement. *Georgia Straight*, May 1–8, 2008.

"Vancouver and Racial Violence (1886–1907)." *British Columbia: One Hundred Years 1871–1971: A Time to Remember*. LP. Gaiety Records—D & L Music, 1971.

Vancouver Daily Province. "Grand Jury's Criticism of Slum Areas Wins Praise of Alderman Gutteridge: Housing Drive To Be Pressed." March 25, 1939.

———. "Vancouver's Slums." April 28, 1939.

Vancouver Redevelopment Study. Vancouver: City of Vancouver Planning Department, 1957.

Wade, Jill. *Houses for All: The Struggle for Social Housing in Vancouver, 1919–50*. Vancouver: University of British Columbia Press, 1994.

Wah, Fred. *Diamond Grill*. Edmonton: NeWest, 1996.

———. *Faking It: Poetics and Hybridity*. Edmonton: NeWest, 2001.

Wenner, Jann S. "John Lennon: The Rolling Stone Interview, Part

One: The Working Class Hero," *Rolling Stone* 74, January 21, 1971. http://www.jannswenner.com/Archives/John_Lennon_Part1. aspx.

West Coast LINE 41, vol. 37, no. 2–3 (2003–04). Special issue, Vidaver, Aaron, ed. "Woodsquat."

Wikipedia: The Free Encyclopedia. http://en.wikipedia.org/ (accessed March 11, 2010).

Winks, Robin W. *The Blacks in Canada: A History*, 2nd ed. Montreal and Kingston: McGill-Queen's University Press, 1997.

INDEX

WAYDE COMPTON is the author of two poetry collections: *49th Parallel Psalm*, shortlisted for the Dorothy Livesay Poetry Prize, and *Performance Bond*, and the editor of *Bluesprint: Black British Columbian Literature and Orature*, all published by Arsenal Pulp Press. He is a founder of Commodore Books and the Hogan's Alley Memorial Project. He lives in Vancouver, where he teaches English composition and literature at Emily Carr University of Art + Design and Coquitlam College.